walking on water

walking on water

READING, WRITING, AND REVOLUTION

DERRICK JENSEN

CHELSEA GREEN PUBLISHING COMPANY
WHITE RIVER JUNCTION, VERMONT

The epigraph on pages 11 and 12 are from *On Becoming a Person* by Carl Rogers.
Copyright © 1961 by Carl R. Rogers. Excerpted and reprinted by permission
of Houghton Mifflin Company. All rights reserved.

Text on page 64 is from *Desert Quartet* by Terry Tempest Williams,
copyright © 1995 by Terry Tempset Williams. Used by permission of
Pantheon Books, a division of Random House, Inc.

The lyrics for "Time" on page 65 are from the album *The Dark Side of the Moon*.
"Time" words and music by Roger Waters, Nichols Mason, David Gilmore, and
Rick Wright. Copyright © 1973 (renewed) Hampshire House Publishing
Corporation, New York, NY. Used by permission.

Designed by Peter Holm, Sterling Hill Productions
Printed in The United States on acid-free, recycled paper

First printing, December 2003

10 9 8 7 6 5 4 3 2 1

Library of Congress Cataloging-in-Publication Data
Jensen, Derrick, 1960-
   Walking on water : reading, writing, and revolution / Derrick
Jensen.
      p. cm.
Includes bibliographical references.
   ISBN 1-931498-48-2
   1. Teaching. 2. Education—Aims and objectives. I. Title.
LB1025.3.J45 2004
371.102—dc22

                                                    2003018242

Chelsea Green Publishing Company
Post Office Box 428
White River Junction, VT 05001
(800) 639-4099
www.chelseagreen.com

contents

School is indeed a training for later life not because it teaches the 3 Rs (more or less), but because it instills the essential cultural nightmare fear of failure, envy of success, and absurdity.

—Jules Henry

a nation of slaves

As is true for most people I know, I've always loved learning. As is also true for most people I know, I always hated school. Why is that?

The answer, obvious to me now, is that I didn't like what I was learning. I don't think my primary problem was with the subjects themselves: I taught myself about numbers before first grade so I could follow baseball statistics, and I was writing plays (albeit short ones) in second grade. It was something deeper.

One of the difficulties we have in thinking or speaking about the problems of our school system is that we presume the primary purpose of school is to help children learn how to read, write, and do arithmetic. This is an understandable mistake, but one we continue to make at our peril. For more is at stake in the process of schooling than mere booklearning or even the development of character. The process of schooling gives children the tools they can—and often must—use to survive after graduating into "the real world," and teaches them what it is to be a member of our culture. Not often enough asked are the questions: What sorts of tools are these? and, What *is it* to be a member of this culture? In other words, we might be well served to ask what sorts of beings we are creating by the process of schooling.

My own primary experience of school was one of tedium. Year after year I sat in the back of the class, watching the second hand move ever so slowly. I can't tell you how many times I calculated the seconds until school was over for the day, the week, the year, thus branding into my mind the importance of arithmetic. When bored I tend to laugh, and almost daily I pinched the insides of my thighs until they turned red, or sometimes bit the inside of my cheek until it was raw, all to keep me from bursting into uncontrollable laughter. I shifted from cheek to cheek on my buttocks, trying to keep my legs from falling asleep. I snuck books into classrooms and read them in my lap. I taught myself American Sign Language in an attempt to communicate silently with a friend in another row, even if for no other purpose than to tell him he looked like a booger. I tested to see how long I could hold my breath. I counted the number of times the teacher said *um* or *okay* in one hour, with the record being a remarkable 215 (I still remember the number as well as the welt I brought up on the inside of my thigh that day). In sum, one of the primary things I learned was how to kill time.

I learned also to wish away my life. I remember a spring day in eighth grade, standing on the football field with a new friend whose name I no longer recollect. I told him I couldn't wait for the next month to be over, when summer vacation would begin. He looked at me, confused, and said to me something he had clearly heard from a parent: "You're wishing away the only thing you've got." I knew immediately he was right, but that didn't alter the fact that I wished it were June instead of May.

What else did I learn? I learned to not talk out of order, and to not question authority—not openly, at least—for fear of losing recess time, or later of losing grade points. I learned to not ask difficult questions of overburdened or impatient teachers, and certainly not to expect thoughtful answers. I learned to mimic the opinions of teachers, and on command to vomit facts and interpretations of those facts gleaned from textbooks, whether I agreed with the facts or interpretations or not. I learned how to read authority figures, give them what they wanted, to fawn and brownnose when expedient. In short, I learned to give myself away.

4

I've talked to friends whose development was similarly shunted (or stunted) by school, though for some the emphatic feeling was anxiety instead of tedium. I am not the only person who twenty years later still dreams anxiously—as I did again about a month ago—that it's the last week of class and I'm frantically preparing for a test on a subject I do not know and do not care about, and for which I've no idea even where the classroom is.

It's not possible to talk about schooling without talking about socialization. It's not possible to talk about socialization without talking about society, and what society values. We hear a lot of talk—a lot of meaningless talk, really—about how terrible it is that high school students cannot locate the United States on a map of the world (which should be easy enough: just look in the center), give the century in which the American Civil War was fought, or name any members of the president's cabinet. We are told that standardized testing must be imposed to make sure students meet a set of standardized criteria so they will later be able to fit into a world that is itself increasingly standardized. Never are we asked, of course, whether it's a good thing to standardize children (sorry, I mean students), knowledge, or the larger world. But none of this—not maps, not dates, not names, not tests—is really the point at all, and to believe so is to fall into the fallacy that school is about learning information, not behaviors.

We hear, more or less constantly, that schools are failing in their mandate. Nothing could be more wrong. Schools are succeeding all too well, accomplishing precisely their purpose. And what is their primary purpose? To answer this, ask yourself first what society values most. We don't talk about it much, but the truth is that our society values money above all else, in part because it represents power, and in part because, as is also true of power, it gives us the illusion that we can get what we want. But one of the costs of following money is that in order to acquire it, we so often have to give ourselves away to whomever has money to give in return. Bosses, corporations, men with nice cars, women with power suits. Teachers. Not that teachers have money, but in the classroom they have what money elsewhere represents: power. We live in a culture that is based on the illusion—and schooling is central to the creation and perpetuation of this illusion—that happiness lies outside of us, and specifically in the hands of those who have power.

Throughout our adult lives, most of us are expected to get to work on time, to do our boss's bidding (as she does hers, and he his, all the way up the line), and not to leave till the final bell has rung. It is expected that we will watch the clock, counting seconds till five o'clock, till Friday, till payday, till retirement, when at last our time will again be our own, as it was before we began kindergarten, or preschool, or daycare. Where do we learn to do all of this waiting?

Also expected is that we will be good citizens, good boys and girls all. We won't question country, God, capitalism, science, economics, history, the rule of law, but in all those areas we will defer—and continue to defer—to experts, just as we were taught. And the experts themselves? It is expected that they will be exquisitely sensitive self-censors, knowing always what or whom to question, what questions to leave unexamined, and most of all which asses to kiss. And none of us, if all goes well, will ever question how these areas—religion, capitalism, science, history, law—trick out in our own lives, even as we give our lives away.

Here are some questions I've been asking lately: What are the effects of schooling on creativity? How well does schooling foster the uniqueness of each child who passes through? Does schooling make children happier? For that matter, does our culture as a whole engender happy children? What does each new child receive in exchange for the so many hours for years on end that she or he gives to the school system? How does school help to make each child who he or she is?

A couple of years ago I was at a public library in Spokane, Washington. A counselor type led a bunch of reluctant teenagers through the front door and to the computer card catalog. There he turned them over to what he must have thought was the hippest of the librarians, a ponytailed young man in a checked flannel shirt. The kids sulked. It was pretty clear they were from a detention center, or rehab, or perhaps had gotten in trouble at school and been sent here as punishment. The librarian pointed to the terminals, then said, "Give me a subject."

No one spoke.

"Anything," he said. "You tell me what you want to read about, and I'll find you a book on it."

From my vantage point at another bank of terminals, I could see that despite himself, one of the guys began to get interested. He was easy to read. *I can look up any subject,* he was thinking, *just like that?* The kid wore baggy jeans. He was Hispanic, with a bandana on his head. He had as much of a goatee as any sixteen-year-old can muster. He started to say something, then stopped. Still no one else spoke. Finally he raised his hand, and said, "You got a book on guns?"

The man with the ponytail just looked at him, so the kid said again, clearly, as if the other were hard of hearing, "Guns."

Everyone laughed. The kid stared for a moment before looking down, and away. I could tell he was wishing he had a gun right then, to blow a hole in the front of the computer. I was wishing I had one to help him.

I saw a blonde girl on the other side raise her hand, and I heard her say, "Whales."

The librarian said, "Whales," and typed it in.

That's why children hate school.

~

I first touched on education in my book *A Language Older Than Words*. Because education was peripheral to that book, I knew someday I'd revisit the subject, and greatly expand on what I wrote there. And because what I *did* say there I said as well as I could, there's an aggregate of probably four or five pages cribbed and reworked from that book sprinkled throughout this one.

~

I have experienced learning, even in a classroom, as liberation. I have taught—*taught* isn't the right word, because I've always considered it my role instead merely to create an atmosphere in which students wish to learn—at a university and at a prison. The original intent of this book—with a working title of *How to Not Teach*—was to sketch my experiences at Eastern Washington University and at Pelican Bay State Prison—experiences that are more similar than one might at first expect—in the hope that someone else might gain from this retelling. I soon realized, however, that to describe my experience in a vacuum would be artificial, and less helpful than if it were embedded in a discussion of the social context that creates our usual experience of schooling. Another way to say this is that before asking whether I or anyone else has been successful in the classroom, we need to ask what we want to accomplish. And before we can rely on our answer to this second question, we need to ask what we are already doing and what we are currently creating by the process of schooling, because that understanding will help us understand—all rhetoric aside—what we *really* want, and will also make clear the stakes involved in the formation of students' characters.

~

Pretend you wish to make a nation of slaves. Or, to put it another way, you wish to procure for your nation's commercial interests a steady supply of workers, and a population pacified enough to not resist the expropriation of their resources. The crudest and probably most common means of facilitating such production is through direct force. Simply capture the workers and haul them to your factories and fields in chains. A slightly more sophisticated approach is to dispossess them, once again usually at gunpoint, then give them the choice of starvation or wage slavery. Alternatively, you can force them to pay taxes or purchase your products, thereby guaranteeing they'll enter the cash economy, meaning, ultimately, that they've got to work in your factories or fields to gain the cash.

The primary drawback of each of these approaches is that the slaves still know they're enslaved, and the last thing you want is to have to put down a rebellion. Far better for them to believe they're free, because then if they're unhappy the fault lies not with you but with themselves.

It all starts with the children. If you don't start young enough, you'll never be able to acculturate them sufficiently so that they disbelieve in alternatives. And if they honestly believe in alternatives—those not delineated by you—they may attempt to actualize them. And then where would you be?

It seems to me that anything that can be taught to another is relatively inconsequential, and has little or no significant influence on behavior. . . . I have come to feel that the only learning which significantly influences behavior is self-discovered, self-appropriated learning. Such self-discovered learning, truth that has been personally appropriated and assimilated in experience, cannot be directly communicated to another. As soon as the individual tries to communicate such experience directly, often with a quite natural enthusiasm, it becomes teaching, and its results are inconsequential. . . . When I try to teach, as I do sometimes, I am appalled by the results, which seem a little more than consequential, because sometimes the teaching seems to succeed. When this happens I find that the results are damaging. It seems to cause the individual to distrust his [or her] own experience, and to stifle significant learning. Hence I have come to feel that the outcomes of teaching are either unimportant or hurtful. When I look back at the results of my past teaching, the real results seem the same—either damage was done, or nothing significant occurred. . . . As a consequence, I realize that I am only interested in being a learner, preferably learning things that matter, that have some significant influence on my own behavior. . . . I find that one of the best, but most difficult ways for me to learn is to drop my own defensiveness, at least temporarily, and to try to understand the way in which [another's] experience seems and feels to the other person. I find that another way of learning is for me to state my own uncertainties, to try to clarify my puzzlements, and thus get closer to the meaning that my experience actually seems to have. . . . It seems to mean letting my experience carry me on, in a direction which appears to be forward, toward goals that I can but dimly define, as I try to understand at least the current meaning of that experience.

—Carl Rogers

how to not teach

It's the first day of class. I walk in, wearing an old suit jacket—the only one I've got—because the department wants the new teaching assistants to look professional. Although the suit is old—old enough to have been worn at my brother's wedding when I was a teenager, later on my disastrous prom date, and not much since—it doesn't look quite so ridiculous as one might think. I haven't gained *that* much weight in the past decade. (Oh, okay, so I have, but the jacket was cavernous in the first place, and now I just don't button it.) Nonetheless, the first thing I do is take it off. I put it on the back of a chair. I look at the college students—some young, fresh off the farm (literally: the school is at the eastern fringe of the Palouse, some of the finest farm country in the West); some foreign students, mainly from Asia; some continuing students much older than I—all sitting in rows facing me. The rows give me a headache. I look around the room, and see a cork bulletin board by the door. The board is filled with advertisements for Visa, Mastercard, vacation specials, and, boldly enough, prewritten term papers. I walk to the back of the room. The students' eyes follow me. "Advertising," I say, "has no place in the classroom." I pull the ads from the wall and throw them in the trash. I walk to the front. Their eyes still follow me. I smile, and the first thing one of them says to me is, "Shouldn't you put all of that into the recycling bin?"

~

I wasn't always comfortable in front of a classroom. At first I was scared. That was years before, when I was twenty-three and going to graduate school only so I could continue my collegiate high jumping career (I broke my foot anyway, and so didn't get to jump). An instructor I knew told me he had a way to get my school paid for: I was to be his teaching assistant for two undergraduate English classes. But before he'd take me on, I had to look up a word in the dictionary. The word was *sinecure*. I'd never heard of it.

Here's what I read. "Sinecure: an office which has revenue without employment; any office or post which gives remuneration without requiring much work, responsibility, etc." It sounded good to me. Even better, I discovered it was a reasonably accurate description of my duties, or lack thereof. I got paid to sit in the back of the class and watch him teach, and then to talk with him for long hours after his evening classes ended (I later learned his marriage was unhappy, and he was perhaps not quite so interested in our philosophical discussions as he was in staying away from home). Occasionally I graded a paper or two, and a couple of times I got up in front of class.

My lectures were more or less disasters. I stammered. I forgot what I was going to say. But the times I didn't forget were, in retrospect, even worse, because I didn't do much more than unthinkingly pass on to the students the speeches my teachers had presumably unthinkingly passed on to me. The students seemed as little moved or informed by these speeches as I had been. Once, I fulminated that they must never use prepositions to end sentences with. Another time I gave a tired talk on spelling. Always absent in all of this—because it wasn't yet present in me, and you can't give what you don't have— was the understanding that the only real job of any teacher, especially a writing teacher, is to help students find themselves. Everything else is either distraction, or at best, window dressing.

~

Here's something I wish I would have told my students. The word *education* (and I mention this derivation in my book *A Language Older Than Words*) comes from the latin root *e-ducere,* meaning "to lead forth" or "to draw out." Originally it was a midwife's term meaning "to be present at the birth of." I would contrast that with the root of the word *seduce,* which is closely related, but with a striking difference. To *educe* is to lead forth; to *seduce* is to lead astray. I wish I had talked about that with those students years ago, and I wish I had suggested that they think about that difference the next weekend. As they approached someone of their preferred gender, perhaps they would have said, "I would like to educe you" (which would have been great if their intended happened to be conversant in Latin, but otherwise might have led the other to say, "Get away from me, you perv!"). More to the point, I wish I had suggested that our departments of education be called, if we were honest, departments of seduction, for that is what they do: lead us away from ourselves.

On second thought, maybe it's best I didn't talk about that. I was having enough trouble talking about prepositions, and spelling. Who knows what sort of trouble I could have gotten into had I begun talking about the relationship between classrooms and seduction.

~

The most important piece of technology in any classroom is the second hand of the clock. The purpose is to teach millions of students the identical prayer: *Please God, make it move faster.*

~

A few years after college, I became a high jump coach at North Idaho College, a junior college in Coeur d'Alene, Idaho. Because self-confidence plays an even more important role in high jumping than in most other sports—if you don't believe you can make a jump, you almost certainly won't, and if you do believe you'll make it, you probably still won't, which means you have to *know* you'll make it such that all self-consciousness disappears—my coaching consisted almost exclusively of praise. This doesn't mean I never gave technical advice. It merely means I was creative in how I gave it, making certain that no matter what we talked about on the surface, the overriding message was the same: *you're an excellent jumper.* For example, I never said, "Todd, your form stinks." Instead, I'd say, "Todd, your leg strength is amazing, because you're popping way up in the air, and your form isn't really helping you. When your form comes together with your leg strength, you're going to be unbeatable." Instead of fixating on his form, he fixated on his leg strength.

And of course I'd never lie. The trick to teaching through praise is that you must never fib. People are so used to criticism and so unused to praise that praise makes them suspicious: If you lie, they'll smell it faster than a fart in a car. It's far better, and far less work, to simply search for the good in the first place and build from there than it is to have to rebuild credibility lost through a demonstrably untrue compliment (and besides, telling the positive truth keeps the focus where it belongs: on your students and their skills, rather than on you and your lack of credibility).

I prohibited my jumpers from saying anything negative about anything within fifty yards of the pit. I'd bait them, asking, for example, how they liked the weather on a drizzly March day, and if they took the bait and complained, I'd make them run a lap. Then they'd have to tell me what they liked about the weather—they in their track shorts, me in my down jacket. At first they complained about the obvious artificiality of this pro-hibition—for which complaint I once again made them run, until they learned to hold their complaints until we got away from the pit—but I knew I was headed in the right direction the first meet with miserable weather. All the other jumpers were complaining about the cold, the wet, the unstable footing for their approach (as I had complained about all these when I was a jumper). The jumpers from North Idaho, on the other hand, were listing ways the weather gave them an advantage: "My approach is slower, so I'm less likely to lose footing on the corner." They fixated on the good.

They also jumped very well. All of my eligible jumpers quali-fied for nationals. All became All-Americans or honorable men-tion All-Americans. One became national champion.

~

Someone asked me once at a talk why I so stress the positive with my students yet am such an unstinting critic of those who run our culture and who are killing the planet. I answered immediately, "Power. If I've got power or authority over someone, it's my responsibility to use that only to help them. It's my job to accept and praise them into becoming who they are. But if I see someone misusing power to harm someone else, it's just as much my responsibility to stop them, using whatever means necessary."

~

Soon enough, we spread through the building, going into all the empty classrooms, ripping down advertisements wherever we found them. For weeks after, students brought in advertisements they'd ripped off the walls of other buildings on campus. They started sealing up postage-paid envelopes to return to advertisers. Recycling bins overflowed.

~

When I entered a classroom for real, and not as a sinecure, many years later, at Eastern Washington University, I immediately changed the name of the course from "Principles of Thinking and Writing" to "Intellectual, Philosophical, and Spiritual Liberation and Exploration for the Fine, Very Fine, and Extremely Fine Human Being." We moved the desks out of rows, and into a circle. As I went around the classroom taking roll, I asked each student what he or she loved. They told me stories of their families, of farming, of their art, of their love for sports. But even more than learning details of their lives, I learned that they were natural storytellers. Just as my jumpers hadn't really needed to be taught how to jump, but rather needed to be led forth into becoming the jumpers they already were (one reason I didn't sweat Todd's form was that I knew I couldn't do much about it anyway), so, too, I realized quickly that my writing students didn't so much need to be taught how to write as they needed to be cheerled into becoming the writers they had inside of them. They knew how and where to start a story, how to include appropriate details, how to make the story lead to a payoff. All of this was there in the first stories they told, of what or whom they loved. They just had to realize the gifts they already possessed. I could not create gifts for them from nothing, but, surely and easily, I could help with this.

~

This, also, is what I say to students on the first day of class: "I once had an instructor—an economics instructor, if you can believe it—

who told me, 'Never believe anything you read, and rarely believe anything you think.' He was one of the best teachers I've ever had."

I stop, then ask, "Have you ever taken a walk down old railroad tracks? And did you keep walking, walking, walking until you decided you were far enough from town? And then did you take your watch from your pocket (if you even bothered to bring a watch), and place it on the tracks? Did you take a dozen steps and still hear its ticking over the rush of blood in your ears? And when a train came by, did you stand to one side and let the wind blow back your hair, stand trembling with fear and excitement until the last car roared past and you could once again breathe?

"Have you ever seen the stars in the desert, or the moon? Have you lain naked in the dew? When did you last walk barefoot in the snow, watch a falling star, or take a bath in a fast cold river? When was the last time you listened to the piper at the gates of dawn? These are more of the best teachers I've ever had.

"But I'll tell you the best. I used to have a dog—an old cocker spaniel—who never seemed to slow down. He ran this way and that, ears flying and tongue flapping. His tail never stopped, no matter what he did. He routinely ignored me, as has every dog I've ever been associated with. The lesson I've learned from dogs has been that rules are meant to be acknowledged, and then ignored. Everything that dog did, he did exuberantly, joyously, with an abundance of life. I can't imagine a better teacher."

A long breath. They aren't sure what to make of me. I'm not sure what to make of them either. I say, "Passion, love, hate, fear, hope. The best writing springs from these sources. Life itself springs from these sources, and what is writing without life? Writing and life. Life and writing. One is the stuff of the other, and the other is the stuff of the one. So by definition this is as much a class in life—in passion, love, fear, experience, relation—as it is in writing. Be warned. If you're here purely for credit, hoping to sleep through yet another quarter of semicolons, diagrammed sentences, and five-paragraph essays, this class will be an incredible drag both for you and for me. If you're not interested in approaching the ragged edge of control where instinct and euphoria set you free from time and consciousness, you would in all honesty be better off in another class. If that's the case do us both a favor and run, don't walk, to my supervisor's office. He and I have an arrangement: I do what I want in the classroom, and he guarantees that if you don't like the style and want to switch, he'll place you elsewhere. And that's okay. My style doesn't work for everybody. And the fact that it doesn't work for everyone is not a reflection on either me or you—it's like having two books on a shelf, one of which is red and the other green. They just don't match. But if you're willing to ride the wave, and let the wave ride you, if you want to write from the gut, from the soul, then reach deep into the tiger's fur and hold on tight, because we're all in for a wild ride."

Nobody moves.

"Since it's my experience that, as Carl Rogers wrote, the only real learning is self-discovered, self-appropriated learning, I won't try to teach you anything. It's my job instead to create an atmosphere where you can teach yourself.

"And one of the skills that is oh-so-necessary in these days of decaying mythologies and rampant corporate and governmental doublespeak is the ability to think critically. To question authority, to question everything. My friend Jeannette Armstrong says, 'We all have cultural, learned behavior systems that have become embedded in our subconscious. These systems act as filters for the way we see the world. They affect our behaviors, our speech patterns and gestures, the words we use, and also the way we gather our thinking. We have to find ways to challenge that continuously. To see things from a different perspective is one of the most difficult things we have to do.'

"She continues, 'I have to constantly school myself in the deconstruction of what I believe and perceive to be the way things are, to continuously break down in my own mind what I believe, and continuously add to my knowledge and understanding. In other words, never to be satisfied that I'm satisfied. That sounds like I'm dissatisfied, but it doesn't mean that. It means never to be complacent and think I've come to a conclusion about things, to always question my own thinking. I always tell my writing class to start with and hold on to the attitude of saying *bullshit* to everything. And to be joyful and happy in that process. Because most of the time it's fear that creates old behaviors and old conflicts. It's not necessarily that we believe those things, but we know them and so we continue those patterns and behaviors because they're familiar.'

"So, it's wonderfully acceptable," I say, "to disagree with me. It's wonderfully acceptable to disagree with anyone. Just be agreeable, at all times respectful, in the way you disagree. Be full of thought, and thoughtful in your disagreement."

Silence.

"Any questions so far?"

A young man raises his hand.

I nod.

He says, "You said the word *bullshit* in class."

"Yes?"

"Will you say that again? I've never heard a teacher say that before."

"Bullshit," I say.

~

Years ago I got into a long conversation with a well-traveled guitarist. He'd played with the best, he said, going back to the sixties.

He'd shared stages with everyone from Carlos Santana to Randy California to Jimi Hendrix to Jimmy Page. But the guitarist who'd taught him the most, he said, was an old blues master he'd met when he was a kid. He'd asked the man to teach him how to play, and the man had responded, "I can teach you everything I know in fifteen minutes. Then you just have to go home and practice for fifteen years."

It's pretty clear to me the same is true for writing, for high jumping, and for life.

Always grab the reader by the throat in the first paragraph, sink your thumbs into his windpipe in the second, and hold him against the wall until the tag line.

—Paul O'Neil

don't bore the reader

t's the second day of class. I come in a couple of minutes late. The students have already moved the chairs out of rows and into a circle. I announce that we have a seating rule. They stare at me, jaws open. After only one day, I'm already used to this response. "The one rule in seating," I say, "is that you can't sit where you sat yesterday. Nor can you sit next to the same people."

"That's two rules," someone says.

"So it is," I respond.

"You said there was only one seating rule."

It's my turn to stare.

They grumble a little as they move to different seats.

The first reason for making this rule is obvious: I want for them to try to see things from a different perspective each day they come in. The second is sneakier, and something I wish my teachers had done for me when I was in school: I want to give the shyer members of the class an excuse to sit next to someone they might be interested in educing, or at least talking to, or at the very least admiring from close-up rather than afar.

"Okay," I say. "Take out paper and pencil. We're going to talk about the rules of writing."

A look of resignation and recognition passes over their faces as they realize that my retitling of the course and my question the day before about what they love were both merely ways to seduce them into thinking this class was something different. The revolution now safely over, they're ready to meet the new boss, who will be, of course, the same as the old boss. They assume student mode, ready to write down what I say so they can regurgitate it back to me later.

"The first rule of writing is: Don't bore the reader."

They write it down.

I continue, "It doesn't matter how important a writer's message is if the book or movie doesn't keep your interest. If you read a book and it's boring, what do you do? If you watch a movie and it's dull, what do you do? Anytime you pick up a book or watch a movie, you could be doing anything else in the world. You could be taking a walk. You could be eating. You could be having a wonderful discussion about what it will take to dismantle civilization."

They nod dutifully. Some take notes.

"You could," I continue, "be having sex."

Pencils stop. I have their attention.

"The same is true for me with the papers you write. I could be doing anything else instead of reading them. So, I have only one requirement for your papers. I don't care what you write about. It can be fiction or nonfiction. I don't care whether I agree or disagree with your opinions."

Blank faces, and I know they don't believe me. Pencils moving.

"But the important thing is this: The papers have to be good enough—interesting enough—that I would rather read them than make love. Is that clear?"

Pencils stop again. Confusion. A woman in her late twenties, sitting in the far corner of the room, issues a single staccato laugh. Having been given implicit permission by her response, the rest of the class begins to laugh, too. They think I'm kidding.

~

The students at Eastern Washington University always laughed when I told them this. Recently I gave a guest lecture to a class at the University of Nebraska. When I mentioned this requirement in my classes—that the papers be better than sex—the students in this class stared at me thoughtfully. Some nodded. I told them their response suggested to me either that they were very good writers, or that they should consider taking a quick trip at the earliest opportunity to eastern Washington.

In my twenties I was for a time a storyteller. I should amend that. I was for a time a terrible storyteller. One problem was that I was still too scared in front of crowds to be any good. But my main problem was that my storytelling was false. I didn't yet understand that in order to write something good, or to tell a good story, I didn't have to invent something fantastic: I simply had to be as much myself as possible. But I did a fair number of festivals, mainly tagging along with a friend, Waddie Mitchell, an excellent and famous cowboy poet. Once, after the last night of a festival in Ann Arbor, Michigan, one of the other tellers, an extraordinary storyteller named Milbre Burch, talked with me through the night. She had me tell her one of my signature stories, and she critiqued it word by word. At one point I used the wrong word to describe something—I called a trowel a spade—and when she corrected me I said (the forty-two-year-old me is horrified to remember these words come out of the twenty-six-year-old me's mouth), "It's just a word."

"Just a word," she replied. "No. You mugged me, as surely as if you had taken my wallet. You mugged me with words, stole a moment of my life. Every time you're on stage, or every time you write something for someone else to read, all the people in the audience, all the people who read your writing, are giving you the honor of time they could be spending elsewhere. You are responsible for every second they give you. You need to give them gifts—including the truth as you understand it to be—commensurate with that every moment."

~

"The question becomes," I say, "how do you keep your readers' interest? What gifts do you give? How do you make it worth their while?"

Nothing. They expect me to answer the questions as well as to ask them.

"What makes you keep watching a movie?"

"Action," someone finally says. It's a guy.

"Action," I repeat. "I'm flipping through the channels at my mom's, and I see some guy peeking around a corner holding a gun, I'm probably going to stick around at least long enough to see what happens. And something has to happen. The rule in westerns, I've heard, is that you have to shoot the deputy in the first ten pages."

This rule has convinced many of my students at prison to write westerns.

"Humor," someone else says.

"Jokes are good," I reply.

Someone else: "Suspense."

"That's a big one. Did anybody see that gawdawful movie *The Vanishing?*"

Thankfully for them, none have.

"I've only seen the European version. I've heard the American version is even worse. It's about a couple on a road trip who stop at a truck stop, and she disappears. He spends the rest of the movie trying to find out what happened to her. Now, the dialog was ludicrous, the acting laughable, and the main character is really an idiot, but I watched the rest of that goddamn movie just so I could find out what happened to her. It was horrid. They got me only with suspense."

Silence, until someone says, "And?"

"And what?"

"And what happened to her?"

"Another thing you can do with suspense," I say, "is take someone almost to the end of a thought or the end of a bit of action, and then jump off to talk about something else. Readers have to then go through all this fairly boring stuff until you finally come back to deliver the goods. You want to keep setting up itches, but never completely scratch one itch until you've got another itch set up."

"What happened to the woman?" the same person asks.

"Okay," I say. "Action, humor, suspense. What else?"

"I like to read the Bible," a woman says.

"Why?" I ask.

"So I can learn about God."

"There's another thing a writer can do to hold your interest: teach you something. It doesn't matter whether it's about God, history, philosophy, life, or how to fix a car. The important thing is that it's got to be what you want and need and are ready to learn."

Silence.

"How about beautiful writing? Great dialog? Those will keep you going. Interesting characters, not just stereotypes, but rounded people revealed by what they do. One reason, by the way, that many movies from the forties and fifties are better than movies today is that a lot of writers back then had already put in time as novelists, and so knew how to draw characters. Today, a lot of writers come out of film school, MTV, or advertising, which means they're a lot better at keeping viewers off-balance with jump cuts and striking images, but they don't know how to write the sort of dialog that would reveal everything you need to know about a character in one perfect sentence. There's a scene late in the movie *Rain Man* where the Dustin Hoffman and Tom Cruise characters are shown going repeatedly up and down escalators. The scenes are striking, but I kept thinking that the same time could have used to teach me about the characters with some sharp dialog."

They seem to get it, but don't say anything.

"What else will keep you interested?"

I know what they're thinking, but no one will say it.

"I'll say it, then. Sex. I think the remote control has added a lot of sex to movies. You're flipping through the channels, and you see some skin. That might be likely to hold you there at least for a moment."

"Depends on whose skin," a student says. Then more silence. I know what else they're thinking, but once again no one will say it.

"Violence. I think it was Charles Dickens who said, 'When in doubt, kill a child.' He's talking about plots here, not real life. But with Charles Dickens, you never know. Years ago I read a philosophy book by Michel Foucault called *Discipline & Punish*. It's essentially an examination of the last five centuries of state response to criminals. It's one of the best written philosophy books I've read. Foucault starts with a graphic description of the torture and execution of someone who'd tried to kill the king. They use red-hot pincers to tear his flesh. They pour boiling oil into the wounds. They tie each arm and leg to a horse and have the horses try to pull him apart. When that doesn't work they hack off his arms and legs. It's horrible and disgusting. And it made me read the damn book. I kept expecting more, but what I got was several hundred pages of philosophy."

"Didn't you feel cheated?" someone asks.

"No, because the philosophy was interesting. If it had been boring, it would have been a cheap trick. But it worked, which I guess by definition means it isn't too cheap a trick."

"Speaking of cheap tricks," the person who keeps asking about *The Vanishing* says, "what happened to the woman?"

"Ah, you've got to watch the movie to find out." Beat. "No, if the movie was any good, I'd make you watch it. But she got kidnapped and buried alive. So does he in the end."

A couple of people say, "Oh, I saw that. It was a great movie."

A student asks, "Does this rule, that writing needs to be better than sex, apply only to books and movies, or to classes as well?"

"It's my job to make these classes interesting enough that you would rather come to class than have sex." They laugh. They don't know I'm serious. "Otherwise, why would you possibly come to class?"

I'd like to say my classes were interesting enough that every student always attended voluntarily, but that wouldn't be quite true. Most students did, and in fact, in every quarter students from previous quarters sometimes wandered in to see how the new classes were going, and to participate in some of their favorite exercises. For a couple of quarters I tried not taking roll, not giving credit for attendance nor taking it away for absence, but there were always one or two people per quarter who would never show up uncoerced. I asked one, "Do you like the class?"

"Yes, I like it a lot."

"But you won't show up unless I take roll."

31

Had he said, "Why should I be in a classroom if I can be out-side?" I may have simply passed him for the class and told him to show up when he felt like it. But he said, "You've got to be high to think I'd show up for any class on my own, even if I like it."

I took roll.

~

"The first rule of writing is . . ."

A chorus: "Don't bore the reader."

"Good. The second rule of writing is: Don't bore the reader."

Someone says, "But that's . . ."

"Exactly. And the third rule of writing is: Don't bore the reader. Now, can anyone guess the fourth and fifth rules?"

~

Teaching at prison really isn't that different from teaching any-where else. The students are just students, the writing just writing. Sure, there are some differences, but they're smaller than one might think. There's a lot more action, for example, in the stories told by writers in prison than there is in stories told by writers at college, and the action is more dramatic. And there are some subtle differences in the way I teach. Because my students in prison are for the most part deprived of "regular" face-to-face romantic relationships, I do not tell them that I want their stories to be better than sex; to do so would only remind them of something they don't get, and in some cases will never get for the rest of their lives. Nor for the same reason do I tell them that their stories must be better for me than a walk in the woods. I tell them their stories must be better than other stories I could read, or movies I could watch. This makes the point without making them feel bad.

Soon after I started working in the prison students told me that they noticed I'd never been scared of them. This was rare, they said, almost unique. Many teachers and others became used to them quickly, but in the beginning seemed terrified that any rapid movement on the part of a classmember could signal a shank.

"But there's no reason for you to hurt me," I said. "Why should I be scared?"

"Exactly," they said. "There's no reason."

That said, I'm not stupid. I don't turn my back on students I don't know, and though I'm always friendly and courteous, I'm also always aware that on my belt is an alarm, which I could hit were I for any reason to become afraid. Guards would come to my rescue. My students do not have that option.

~

The foundation of my work in the classroom remains the same for both college and prison, which is to respect and love my students into becoming who they are.

Not all students appreciate my efforts. This is as true at the university as it is in prison, and as it would be, presumably, on the streets and in homes. A couple of years ago a new student came to one of my classes at the prison. I quickly discovered that he was an extraordinary writer. I'll never forget a line he used in a poem to describe a hit man for a gang, as "a wicked chemist mixing metal with flesh." He was there for one class, and then I left on a book tour. When I returned, his yard was locked down, so I didn't see him for many months. Finally they came off lockdown, and next class I saw a tall slender man who looked familiar. I asked him if he was the one who wrote that line about mixing metal with flesh. He looked at me out of the corners of his eyes, and said yes.

I said, "I've been telling people all over the country what a great writer you are. It's a wonderful line."

He smiled. That was one of the few times he seemed to enjoy the class. For the next year or two he was pretty standoffish. He would read his own poems and stories, which were generally excellent, but that was for the most part the extent of his participation. I knew, and I think other people did also, that he didn't much like the class. Then one day he told us what bothered him: "I'm really sick of you babying us. You may as well just bring out the diapers. All you ever do is tell us what good writers we are. Well, the truth is that some of the writers in here suck. Their work is terrible, and you never tell them that."

"I give suggestions," I said. "And if people seem receptive to the suggestions, and if they use them to improve their writing, I give more. If they're not receptive, I'm not going to give advice where it's not wanted."

"But you never tell us what's wrong."

"If you want me to be more aggressive in my suggestions about your work, I'm happy to do that."

"Oh, I'm not talking about my own writing. My writing is fine, and it doesn't mean that much to me anyway. There are some other people in here, though, that you need to talk to. Their writing sucks, and you need to tell them to stop wasting everybody's time, including their own."

He was primarily referring, it seemed clear to me, to one of my favorite students, who came every week, was pleasant, wrote a lot, had a gift for coming up with plots, and, from my perspective most important of all, was teachable. When we first started working together his pieces were closer to outlines than stories. I suggested he put in details to show us, for example, the innocent person actually finding the money from the bank robbery, instead of just saying, "He went for a walk and found a bag with $1 million." What, I asked, does the bag look like? What does he feel when he opens it? Is he nervous? Does he even *think* about giving it back? That last question was met by all with a look that let me know they considered me an idiot. The next week he returned with a seventy-page rewrite containing such details as *precisely* what the guy who found the bag had for breakfast (which started at 7:23), including how many sausages, how many eggs, how each egg was cooked, and so on. It was, by his own admission, a bit much. So we had him cut back. He listened and learned, and that made me happy.

I defended this student publicly.

The other fellow continued to push. We ran out of time.

I came back the next week and said I needed to make something clear. "Nobody," I said, "is allowed to disrespect my students. That includes the students themselves. You're not allowed to disrespect other people in this class, and you're not allowed to disrespect yourselves."

Most students seemed fine with this. I went around the class, asking each person if he wanted to talk about it. One student said he didn't agree with my philosophy of teaching by praise. He said, "If I'm going to improve, I need to know what my weaknesses are as a writer."

I responded, "Do you know what your strengths are as a writer?"

"No."

"Well, after we find out what your strengths are, your weaknesses will be obvious. Doesn't it make more sense to find and develop your strengths first?"

He agreed.

And so it went, until we finally got to the person who had raised the original complaint. He said, "We're convicts. We aren't like other people. We're not like college students you have to put diapers on. We've done terrible things, and some of us are pretty awful people. We need to have you tell us what's wrong with us."

I was furious, not so much at him as at all the people in his life who had convinced him they were taking care of him when they told him what was wrong with him, and at the entire culture founded on this lack of acceptance and nurturance, this lack of respect, this constant wearing away at people's capacity for self-love. I thought of the bumper sticker I saw once: "Those who fear to follow their own dreams will attempt to destroy yours."

I slammed my hand on the table.

Some of the students recoiled.

I said—with voice sharper than I can ever remember it being—"I don't care what you've done. I don't care if you've fucked your mother and killed your best friend. I don't care how anybody treats you outside this room. I don't even care how you treat each other outside this room. I can't control any of that. But in this room you are all human beings, and you will be treated with respect. And you will treat one another with respect. That is not negotiable."

He left. We continued with class. I haven't heard from him since. I suspect he's still writing very good material. Maybe someday I'll see him again. Maybe not.

~

It should surprise us less than it does that the educational system destroys students' souls. From the beginning, that has been the purpose. Don't take my word on this: Take it from the people who set up the system. In 1888 (and I'm indebted to the great website The Memory Hole and the great educator and writer John Taylor Gatto for collecting these quotes on the primary purpose of industrial education), the Senate Committee on Education, nervous about the high quality of education provided by nonstandardized, localized schools (where—the horror! the horror!—teachers actually taught students to think for themselves!), reported, "We believe that education is one of the principal causes of discontent of late years manifesting itself among the laboring classes."

Industrial educators set out to rectify this problem. How? As industrial educator and philosopher John Dewey said, "Every teacher should realize he is a social servant set apart for the maintenance of the proper social order and the securing of the right social growth."

Next questions: What are the proper social order and the right social growth? In 1906, Elwood Cubberly, who later became dean of education at Stanford, gave his answers: Schools should be factories "in which raw products, children, are to be shaped and formed into finished products . . . manufactured like nails, and the specifications for manufacturing will come from government and industry."

Then in 1906, the Rockefeller Education Board, major backer of the movement for compulsory public schooling, gave its reasons for putting its money into that movement: "In our dreams . . . people yield themselves with perfect docility to our molding hands. The present educational conventions [i.e., the development of children's intellects and characters in homes and local schools] fade from our minds, and unhampered by tradition we work our own good will upon a grateful and responsive folk. We shall not try to make these people or any of their children into philosophers or men of learning or men of science. We have not to raise up from among them authors, educators, poets or men of letters. We shall not search for embryo great artists, painters, musicians, nor lawyers, doctors, preachers, politicians, statesmen, of whom we have ample supply. The task we set before ourselves is very simple . . . we will organize children . . . and teach them to do in a perfect way the things their fathers and mothers are doing in an imperfect way."

Those in charge could not have been clearer. William Torrey Harris, U. S. commissioner of education from 1889 to 1906, wrote: "Ninety-nine [students] out of a hundred are automata, careful to walk in prescribed paths, careful to follow the prescribed custom. This is not an accident but the result of substantial education, which, scientifically defined, is the subsumption of the individual."

Finally, bringing this around not only to students' relationships to themselves but to the land, Harris also stated, "The great purpose of school can be realized better in dark, airless, ugly places. . . . It is to master the physical self, to transcend the beauty of nature. School should develop the power to withdraw from the external world."

No wonder we all hate school.

And the fact that we do hate school is a very good thing. It means we're still alive.

I wanted only to try to live in accord with the promptings which came from my true self. Why was that so very difficult?

—Hermann Hesse

who are you?

There's really only one question in life, and only one lesson. This question is whispered endlessly to us from all directions. The moon asks it each night, as do the stars. It's asked by drops of rain that cling to the soft ends of cedar branches, and by teardrops that cluster at the fold of your nose or the edge of your mouth. Frogs, flowers, stones, pieces of broken plastic, all ask this of each other, of themselves, and of you. The question: Who are you? The lesson: We're born or sprouted or hatched or congealed or we fall from the sky, we live, and then we die or are worn away or broken or disperse into a river, lake, or sea, ripples flowing outward to bounce back from the far shore. And in the meantime, in that middle, what are you going to do? How are you going to find, and *be*, who you are? Who are you, and what are you going to do about it?

If modern industrial education—and more broadly industrial civilization—requires "the subsumption of the individual," that is, the conversion of vibrant human beings into "automata," that is, into a pliant workforce, then the most revolutionary thing we can do is follow our hearts, to manifest who we really are. And we are in desperate need of revolution, on all scales and in all ways, from the most personal to the most global, from the most serene to the most wrenching. We're killing the planet, we're killing each other, and we're killing ourselves.

And still our neighbors—hummingbirds, craneflies, huckleberries, the sharp cracking report of the earthquake that shakes you awake in your bed—ask us, who are you, who are you in relation to each of us, and to yourself?

Our current system divorces us from our hearts and bodies and neighbors, from humanity and animality and embeddedness in the world we inhabit, from decency and even the most rudimentary intelligence. (How smart is it to destroy your own habitat? Who was the genius who came up with the idea of poisoning our own food, water, and air?) I've heard defenders of this system say that following one's heart is not a good enough moral compass, that Hitler was following his heart when he tried to conquer the world, tried to rid the world of those he deemed unworthy. But Hitler was no more following his heart than are any of the rest of us who blindly contribute to a culture that is accomplishing what Hitler desired but could not himself bring to completion. The truth is—as I have shown elsewhere, exhaustively and exhaustingly—that it is only through the most outrageous violations of our hearts and minds and bodies that we are inculcated into a system where it can be made to make sense to some part of our twisted and torn psyches to perpetuate a way of being based on the exploitation, immiseration, and elimination of everyone and everything we can get our hands on.

Within this context, the question the whole world asks at every moment cannot help but also be the most dangerous: Who are you? Who are you, really? Beneath the trappings and traumas that clutter and characterize our lives, who are you, and what do you want to do with the so-short life you've been given? We could not live the way we do unless we avoided that question, trained ourselves and others to avoid that question, forced others to avoid placing that question in front of us, and in fact attempted to destroy those who do.

As we see.

It is nearing the end of the first week of class, and I have a question. "If you were suddenly given more money than you could imagine, say a million dollars, would you stay in school?"

Someone says, "I can imagine a lot more than a million."

"Okay, three."

"More."

"Don't get greedy. Now the question: Would you stay in school?"

"You must be crazy." Someone else asks what I've been smoking. Nobody in the class would stay in school. I've asked this question for several years now, and maybe five or six students total have said they would stay.

We talk about what they would do instead. Many would travel. Some would stay home and watch television. Some would throw elaborate parties. Many would make sure their parents, siblings, and friends never have to enter the wage economy. Many would buy their parents a house. A few—especially older, returning students—say that with the exception of quitting school, they wouldn't change much about their lives.

"Would you get or keep a job?"

They laugh. No one says *yes*.

"Okay, you've got all this money, and the next day you go to the doctor for a regular checkup. You discover you have the dreaded *Love Story* disease, which means you'll live for a year with no symptoms of illness—looking great all the time, by the way—but at the end of that time you'll suddenly die. What will you do?"

"Get a second opinion."

I laugh. "It's the same as the first."

They think about it.

"Would you stay in school?"

Of course not.

"If you only had a limited amount of time to live—which is of course the case—would you get a job?"

Of course not. Again, many would travel. Many would spend time with families. Several say they'd have lots of sex. One woman says she'd have a child. Some think that because the child would soon be motherless she's not acting in the child's interest, but others support her decision. A few would learn how to skydive (and on day 366 would skip the parachute). One says that on the final day he'd walk into the (moving) propeller of an airplane, just so he'd have a dramatic exit. A couple would spend the year at hospitals searching for a cure.

When the responses begin to slow, a student asks, thoughtfully, "What's the point of doing this exercise here in class?"

I think a moment, shrug, and say, "To have fun."

He seems to accept that. Someone else asks what I would do differently, if I had the money but no disease.

"Not a damn thing," I say.

"Nothing?"

"Maybe I'd go out to eat more; I'm a wretched cook. And if I had enough money I'd buy land and set it aside so it can recover."

A woman shyly raises her hand. I look at her and nod. She says, softly, "Don't you think you could buy a new jacket, one that fits?"

Someone else says, "And do something about those shirts. Where do you shop, Value Village?"

"Well, actually . . ."

Many of them agree that even if *they* were to win this money and not I, that they would buy me stylin' clothes. They give great detail. When they finally have me properly outfitted, someone asks, "And what if you had only a year to live?"

"I'd write nonstop. I've got a list of books in me, and I don't want to die with a couple of them still there."

"Would you do anything special on the last day?"

"Yeah," I reply. "I'd strap on explosives and head to the nearest dam. That would be the least I could do for the river, and for the salmon."

~

At a talk I gave recently a woman asked what she should say to her fifteen-year-old son, who, although he's very loving (or perhaps *because* he's very loving) hates school, hates the wage economy, hates the culture. She didn't want to tell him to get a job, and was having a hard time convincing herself to tell him to stay in school. I flailed, and my mind began to lock up. I could manage nothing better than, "It's a difficult situation. You want to teach children responsibility but within our culture responsibility has been defined as going to school, as getting a job. As being a slave. Given these constraints, how do you teach responsibility? I don't know."

I took a breath, and before I could continue, another woman in the audience, my old friend Carolyn Raffensperger, a wonderful activist and thinker, asked if she could give a try. I nodded, and she said, "One of the most important things we can do is help young people find their way to be in service to something larger than themselves. Normally the only reason kids go to college or graduate school—and, in Wes Jackson's words, the only real major offered—is upward mobility. But we fail to teach our children that service to something greater than themselves is far more likely to lead to a joyful and satisfying life, and one that is environmentally rich."

The woman looked at her intently, as did most of the other people in the room.

Carolyn continued, "It all starts with the question: 'What's the biggest and most important problem I can solve with my gifts and skills?' Even to form a preliminary answer to that question is to begin to define an appropriate—and fun—path."

This made me think of what some of the ancient Greek philosophers called the point of life: *eudaimonia*. It's commonly translated as *happiness,* but I believe a more accurate translation would be *fittingness:* how well your actions match your gifts, match who you are. My understanding of it is that after we die, we spend a hundred lifetimes being treated how we treated others here on earth, after which we go back into the pool of those to be reborn. When our turn comes we decide who will be our parents and what will be our gifts, our purpose. Just before hopping back to this side we drink something that causes us to forget. And here we are. It becomes our task in this world to remember our gifts, our task, and to realize them, with the help of guiding spirits, or daimons. Thus *eudaimonia,* which literally means "having a good guardian spirit."

Carolyn continued, "After college and graduate school I didn't know what else to do with my life, so I thought I'd go to law school. Basically more upward mobility. I took the LSAT, and scored rock bottom. That's probably a good thing, because if I'd gone, I probably would've been a perfect subject for lawyer jokes. But later I got this sense that I *had* to go to law school so I could work for environmental protection. This time I scored in the upper 3 percent. I was the same person, but now it was the right thing for me to do. I had the right motivation. When people know what problem they can solve using the gifts that are unique to them in all the world, they often know what they need to do next."

I was asked to give a talk to the students at a boys boarding school, grades eight to twelve. I was scared, far moreso than at prison. I told the boys that, and I told them why: When I was in junior high or high school and was forced to attend all-school assemblies, I would sit in the back of the auditorium, hands in my pockets flipping off whomever was giving the talk, just on principle. I asked them to show me their hands. They did and laughed.

I had long agonized over what I should say to them—how I could manifest the first rule of writing or speaking, and especially what gifts I could give to them that would be worth the honor of their time—and finally decided that as usual, when all else fails I should tell the truth. I said I was going to tell them some things I wish someone would have told me when I was their age.

"I guess the first thing I wish someone would have told me is that it's okay to hate school, that it's really crazy to expect people to sit motionless and to pretend to be interested as you bore them out of their skulls, and it's even more crazy to expect them to like it." The boys perked up. So did the administrators, but I suspect for different reasons.

"The only thing that got me through school was daydreaming. I spent all of eighth grade in the batter's box in the seventh game of the World Series. Two outs, bottom of the ninth, down by two, runners on first and second, the count is 0-2. The pitcher hangs a curveball over the plate and BAM! There it goes over the left field fence. Okay, so that got rid of about fifteen seconds. Again, it's game seven of the World Series. Two outs, bottom of the ninth. . . . I spent ninth grade repeatedly winning the NBA championship with a turnaround fadeway at the buzzer. You may have heard of me. In tenth grade it was a fingertip catch in the endzone to win the Super Bowl. I never did sink as low as hockey." (A few years ago I forgot where I was and told that joke in Wisconsin; I was at a Buddhist retreat center, and I don't think you can say you've lived until you've been chased down the street by a bunch of pacifists waving hockey sticks.) "After football, I cut right to the chase and spent my junior and senior years of high school and all of college fantasizing about putting plastic explosives under teachers' desks, as well as the desk of anyone who committed that most unpardonable of all sins, asking a question with less than three minutes left in class."

The boys were cheering. Judging from their faces, some of the administrators were wishing for some plastic explosives themselves.

"The next thing I wish someone would have said to me is that things will get better, especially if you take charge of your own life. At my high school graduation the valedictorian said we would someday look back on these days as the best of our lives. The first thing I thought was, *Boom, there goes the whole stage into a thousand pieces,* but right after that I thought, if this is really as good as it gets, I may as well kill myself right now. But things get better. Junior high stunk. High school stunk. College stunk. The twenties were hard, maybe as bad as school, because it took that long to recover from my earlier schooling and begin to see and think and feel for myself. To teach myself how to think, and how to *be* in the world. But the thirties were good, because by then I had an idea of who I actually am, and I began to live it. And so far the forties are grand. (Thank you very much, Derrick, you've just condemned us to at least fifteen more years of hell.) So don't give up. Things get better. So far as we know, you have only one life, and there's almost nothing more worth fighting for than to figure out what you want—not what you've been told you want by parents or teachers or pastors or advertisers or army recruiters or people who write books and then come sit on this stage and tell you their teenage fantasies about blowing up their schools, but what *you* want—and then pursuing that if it takes you to the ends of the earth and to the end of your own life.

"The third thing I wish someone would have said to me is that

I shouldn't be such a wimp, that I should go ahead and ask the other person out."

The looks on their faces told me this was advice they could use.

I told them that the last thing my mother said to me as I got on a plane to California for the summer between my junior and senior years in high school was, "Make sure she's eighteen," and I told them that was the best thing she could have said to a very shy, very unsure young man who had never been on a date (a description, by the way, that also fit nearly all of my friends). There's something else I wish I had told them, but I did not because the language didn't come to me until later, and that is that I regret my mistakes of timidity more than those of recklessness; actions undone more than actions done. Regrets have never come from following my heart into or out of intimacy, no matter the pain involved, but when, because of fear, I didn't enter or leave when I should have. Regrets have come when fear kept me from my heart. I wish I had told them that this has been true not just with women, but with everything.

I told them about high jumping. Although I've always loved high jumping, I was too afraid to jump competitively until I was a sophomore in college. That year, the coach discovered me messing around on the pit and convinced me to compete. I eventually broke the school record and won the conference championship, but then graduated and ran out of time. Because I'd been too fearful to begin jumping sooner, I'll never know, I told them, how good I could have been. I vowed not to allow that to happen with my life: When I run out of time, I want to have done what I wanted, and what I could.

I also told them, "I sometimes think timidity is destroying the planet as surely as are greed, militarism, and hatred; I now see these as aspects of the same problem. Those in power couldn't commit routine atrocities if the rest of us hadn't already been trained to submit. The planet is being killed, and when it comes time for me to die, I don't want to look back and wish I'd done more, been more radical, more militant in its defense. I want to live my life as if it really matters, to live my life as if I'm alive, to live my life as if it's real."

I took a breath.

"And I want to apologize, just as people in the generation before mine should have apologized to me, for the wreckage of a world we're leaving you. The people of my generation are passing on to you the social patterns and structures, the ways of being and thinking, the physical artifacts themselves that are killing the planet. We're blowing it, badly, and you'll suffer for it. I'm so very sorry.

"Which brings me to the next thing I wish someone had told me. This one would have saved me years of distress. You're not crazy, the culture is crazy. If it seems insane to you that our culture is systematically dismantling the ecological infrastructure of the planet, yet we pay less attention to that than we do to professional sports (Go Mariners!), that's because it *is* insane. If it seems senseless to you that our culture values money and economic productivity over human and nonhuman lives, that's because it *is* senseless. If it seems crazy to you that most people spend most of their waking hours working jobs they'd rather not do, that's because it *is* crazy. There's nothing wrong with you for thinking these things. In fact it means you're still alive.

"I wish also that someone would have told me—one hundred times if that was what it took for me to hear it—that it's okay to be happy, it's okay to live your life exactly the way you want it. It's okay to not get a job. It's okay to *never* get a job. It's okay to find what makes you happy and then to fight for it. To dedicate your life to discovering who you are."

My time was up. The boys started yelling. Some rushed the

stage (I could tell that some administrators considered doing this, too, though once again I suspect for different reasons). A tall, slender boy asked, eagerly, "Does all of this mean we never have to do anything we don't want? Does it mean it will all be easy?"

"It will be very hard. You'll make a million mistakes, and you'll pay for them all, one way or another. That's the only way you learn, or at least it's the only way I learn. But the hard parts will be *your* hard parts, they won't be hard parts other people have imposed on you for their own reasons, or maybe for no reason at all. And your ownership of them—your responsibility to and for them—makes all the difference in the world."

It is our fate, if we never had the chance to rebel, to live the absurdity of never having experienced a self of our own.

—Arno Gruen

If they give you lined paper, write the other way.

(I don't know who first said this. It might have beeen Ray Bradbury, William Carlos Williams, e.e. cummings, or Juan Ramón Jiménez.)

the most important writing exercise

The sixth rule of writing is different," I say. "It is: Show, don't tell."

Pencils move across papers.

"How many of you have ever cried while reading a book?"

Many, including a surprising number of guys, raise their hands. I ask which books. *Old Yeller* wins hands down.

"What is it, really, that you're crying about? Books are nothing more than squiggles of ink on paper. Yet they move us, make us laugh or cry or change our lives. How do they do that?"

I wasn't expecting an answer.

"And how do movies do it? You see Bruce Willis hanging from a cliff, and you're scared he's going to die. Now, you know there's a mattress about five feet below him, and you also know that Bruce Willis isn't going to die, since he's in seven other movies this year, but you're still nervous. How does that work?

"Before we can answer that, we need to bring in another piece of the puzzle, which is that by far the best teacher is experience. I learn much better from my own mistakes than another's. But by definition, when you read something or when you watch a movie, you're not experiencing it yourself; you're experiencing it only vicariously, *through* the participants. So how do filmmakers get you to feel scared when Bruce Willis hangs from a cliff? By getting you to identify with his character. And how do they get you to identify with his character? By having you, insofar as possible, participate in his experiences. And how do they do *that*? By describing those experiences as accurately as possible; by taking you along with him for the ride: in essence by putting not Bruce Willis but *you* in that situation."

They're with me.

I say, "Let's do an exercise. Pretend I'm from Mars."

They have no problem with this one.

"We Martians have no emotions. We feel the same things as you physically, but not emotionally. I can feel pressure in my skin, but I cannot feel love. You may at some point have dated someone like this. Now, to help me understand you Earthlings, I would like for you to tell me, for example, what anger feels like."

Silence for a while, till someone volunteers, "It feels like I'm mad."

"I don't get that either."

"Okay, furious."

"Same thing."

Someone else, "It feels like I'm going to explode."

"Like you've eaten one too many wafer-thin mints, or like your skin is stretching out like a balloon, or like you've just asked a question with less than three minutes left in class?"

A third person: "It feels like I want to punch someone."

"What does that feel like? Where do you feel it? What does anger feel like inside your temples, in your neck, in your shoulders, behind your eyeballs, on the backs of your knees?"

I see understanding in their eyes. A woman says, "My shoulders hunch. The muscles along the top get really tight."

Another: "I clench my jaws, grind my teeth."

Another: "My eyes squint. I feel pressure behind my eyes."

Another: "I start to sweat."

"Where?" I ask.

"A drop runs down each side of my ribs."

"Oh," I say. "These are all *so* good. I can feel them."

We make our way next through fear, and then through love.

They make me define what kind of love, because, they say, it feels different to love a new partner than an older one, to love either of those than a parent, to love a parent than a dog, to love a dog than the land where you live. I'm glad they force rigor in my definition. I say, "Love for a boyfriend or girlfriend just at the stage where you know the other reciprocates your feelings, but you aren't yet settled into the relationship."

They forget everything we've learned so far. Someone says, "It feels like walking on clouds."

"You can do that on Earth? We can't do that on Mars. I think there were some clouds in the sky. Let's go outside and you can show me."

"It feels like everything is great in the world."

"What does that feel like?"

Again, understanding in their eyes. They describe the physical sensations, sometimes veering, it must be admitted, into a particularity of detail that leaves me blushing, yet also sometimes describing love in terms not dissimilar from fear.

I say, "Okay, let's go in a different direction. I want you to describe anger to me again. But now I want you to pretend you're making a movie, which means you can't go inside the person to describe how anger feels. You have to show actions from the outside."

They stare at me blankly.

I slam my open hand on a desk and spit, "God *damn* it!" I frown. I stalk around the center of the room. They recoil. They're very sorry, whatever it is they may have done wrong. I say, "No, that's what I mean. Show it. I dated this woman years ago who'd more or less constantly pick fights with me. It was annoying, but not a big deal, unless she was really mad. And how did she show that? I learned pretty quickly that if she bit her lower lip, nodded, and looked off to the side, I was in big trouble."

Somebody says, "When I get mad I get really quiet, and my voice gets very steely."

Someone else: "My whole body starts to shake, and I ball up my fists."

They continue like this. An interesting difference I note between my students at the prison and my students at the university is that the examples chosen by students at the prison are usually more overt: thrown chairs versus hostile looks. I draw no conclusions from this. I simply observe it.

With this exercise, I hope to get my students to pay attention to details. Paying attention to the proper details is a fundamental lesson of life (try driving in busy traffic without discerning which details are and are not important), and it's probably *the* fundamental lesson of writing (you constantly need to choose which details to include to take the reader with you and which to leave out so as not to bore the reader senseless; most people, for example, defecate at least once per day, yet there's rarely a compelling reason to show this to your audience).

I ask my students to write a description. I want them to include a dark room, a little bit of light, a musical instrument, and dust. I'd like to say these prompts are the result of intensive thought, and that they're designed to play off each other to produce the best possible writing, but the truth is that they're the first things I think of. I ask them to include all five senses. They can put in a plot or not as they choose. The only thing I care about is that I am there: If it's your grandmother's attic in late June at the edge of the Palouse west of Spokane, I want to smell the newly-mown hay; if it's a skanky bar at four in the morning, I want to smell the stale beer and cigarette smoke.

They write. The stories are good. I'm glad.

~

This brings us to the Stephen King corollary to the show, don't tell rule. It is this: Get specific. Stephen King is one of the best at providing specific rather than abstract details, and using those specific details to draw in the reader. He rarely has just any old car in his books: instead it might be "an old Citroën sedan." Any old businessman doesn't go to lunch at just any old place. Instead, as in *Salem's Lot:* "The town whistle went off with a great twelve-second blast, ushering in lunch hour at all three schools and welcoming the afternoon. Lawrence Crockett, the Lot's second selectman and proprietor of Crockett's Southern Maine Insurance and Realty, put away the book he had been reading *(Satan's Sex Slaves)* and set his watch by the whistle. He went to the door and hung the 'Back at One O'Clock' sign from the shade pull. His routine was unvarying. He would walk up to the Excellent Café, have two cheeseburgers with the works and a cup of coffee, and watch Pauline's legs while he smoked a William Penn."

Sometimes in response to this corollary, students say, "But I want my writing to be universal. I want it to speak to everyone."

I tell them that, first, it's impossible to speak to everyone; and second, one of the best ways to reach as many people as possible is by getting them, once again, to experience what you are trying to convey, and one of the best ways to do this is by giving them images they can hang on to. Having read the previous paragraph, I'm there in the Excellent Café with Lawrence, staring at Pauline's legs.

There's a deeper point to be made here, however, having to do with the specificity of everything. One of the great failings of our culture is the nearly universal belief that there can be anything universal. We as a culture take the same approach to living in Phoenix as in Seattle as in Miami, to the detriment of all of these landscapes. We believe that students can be given standard lesson plans and standard tests, universally applied, to the detriment of all of these students. We turn living wild trees into standardized two-by-fours. We turn living fish into fish sticks. We turn living carrots into carrot sticks. But every carrot is different from every other carrot. Every fish is different from every other fish. Every tree is different from every other tree. Every student is different from every other student. Every place is different from every other place. If we are ever to remember what it is to be human beings, and if we are ever to hope to begin to live sustainably in place (which is the only way to live sustainably), we will have to remember that specificity is *everything*. It's the only thing we've got. In this moment, I'm not abstractly writing: I'm writing these specific words on this specific piece of paper using this specific pen, lying on this specific bed next to this specific cat. There is nothing apart from the particular. Now, I can certainly generate abstract notions of writing or humanity or cities or nature or the world, but they're not real. What is real is immediate, present, particular, specific. That's true in life. It's true in writing. And writing is as good a place as any to start.

~

My students nearly always describe instruments they've seen in places they've been: a contraband harmonica in a prison cell, a piano in a church, a violin in the basement of a childhood home. I next ask them to take me to a beach. I don't care about anything, I say, except that if the beach is hot, I want for my feet to hurt when the story is read aloud. If the beach is in southern California, I want to smell the coconut oil. If it's in Alaska I want to smell the dead fish. Again, they write. The pieces are good. They describe beaches they've seen, beaches they've sat on, beaches they've played football on. Writing's not so hard, I say. Just remember places you've been, things you've done, and describe them to me. I really want to hear.

They like it. Nearly everyone likes to be listened to. And they all certainly have stories to tell, things to say.

～

It's my favorite day of class. It's early in the second week. A couple of students have shown up from previous quarters, and the new students suspect something's up. I've brought a CD player, a pile of CDs, and a pile of books. I say, "Normally when I ask you a question, I'm not so much looking for a specific answer. I just want to know what you think. But I'm going to ask you something right now, and I'm definitely fishing. Ready?"

Nods all around.

"What's the attraction of rock 'n' roll?"

They freeze, trying to read my mind for the answer instead of finding their own.

"Is it long-haired men in tight leather pants?" I ask. "Or maybe it's those flourescent green bracelets. How about stepping over someone puking on his shoes? Maybe it's the intellectual content of the songs."

We all agree it's none of those, not even, "If there's a bustle in your hedgerow, don't be alarmed now, it's just a spring clean for the May Queen."

"How about this, then? Power. Passion. Energy."

They like it.

"When Jimi Hendrix destroyed a guitar, he didn't gingerly pluck off each string. He smashed it to bits. When Pete Townsend windmilled, he wouldn't flick his wrist, but he'd put his whole body into it. When Keith Moon destroyed a drumset, he wouldn't just tip it carefully." I delicately tip over a chair-desk combo. It falls with a thud. "Instead he'd rip it apart." I grab the desk, throw it spinning toward the ceiling. It crashes back down.

I say, "There are a hundred people inside each of us who can write. There's the bitter old man, and the lonely old woman. The happy old woman or man tired but satisfied with life. The ecstatic young man, the gleeful little girl. The angry woman. They all have strong opinions, and they're all inside each one of us. Unfortunately, the only one who can't write is the one we wear on our faces all the time. The polite one. The bland one. The one who wants approval. The one who wants a grade. The one who hedges every strong opinion, every strong impulse. That one can't write worth a damn."

I take a breath.

"Writing is really very easy," I say. "Tap a vein and bleed onto the page. Everything else is just technical. Or if you don't want to do that, you can, as Gene Fowler wrote, stare at a blank piece of paper until drops of blood form on your forehead."

I rush to the chalkboard, write in bold letters, "Let go!" I stalk to the CD player, and turn it on. It's Tommy Bolin's "Post Toastee." I turn it up to just below where the speakers distort, and go back to the chalkboard. I write, "No! Really let go!" I start to head back to the CD player, then spin and write on the board, "No! *Really* let go!"

~

Back to the player. I turn it down just enough so they can hear me, and I begin to read, from Edward Abbey's *Desert Solitaire*: "Do not jump into your automobile next June and rush out to the Canyon country hoping to see some of that which I have attempted to evoke in these pages. In the first place, you can't see anything from a car; you've got to get out of the goddamned contraption and walk, better yet crawl, on hands and knees, over the sandstone and through the thornbush and cactus. When traces of blood begin to mark your trail you'll see something, maybe. Probably not. In the second place most of what I write about in this book is already gone or going under fast. This is not a travel guide but an elegy. A memorial. You're holding a tombstone in your hands. A bloody rock. Don't drop it on your foot—throw it at something big and glassy. What do you have to lose?"

I toss aside the book and pick up another, Dalton Trumbo's *johnny got his gun*: "If you [politicians and CEOs and patriots] make a war if there are guns to be aimed if there are bullets to be fired if there are men to be killed they will not be us. They will not be us the guys who grow wheat and turn it into food the guys who make clothes and paper and houses and tiles . . . and shovels and automobiles and airplanes and tanks and guns oh no it will not be us who die. It will be you. It will be you—you who urge us on to battle you who incite us against ourselves you who would have one cobbler kill another cobbler you who would have one man who works kill another man who works you who would have one human being who wants only to live kill another human being who wants only to live. Remember this. Remember this well you people who plan for war. Remember this you patriots you fierce ones you spawners of hate you inventers of slogans. Remember this as you have never remembered anything else in your lives. We are men of peace we are men who work and we want no quarrel. But if you destroy our peace if you take away our work if you try to range us one against the other we will know what to do. If you tell us to make the world safe for democracy we will take you seriously and by god and by Christ we will make it so. We will use the guns you force upon us we will use them to defend our very lives and the menace to our lives does not lie on the other side of a nomansland that was set apart without our consent it lies within our own boundaries here and now we have seen it and we know it. Put the guns into our hands and we will use them. Give us the slogans and we will turn them into realities. Sing the battle hymns and we will take them up where you left off. Not one not ten not ten thousand not a million not ten millions not a hundred millions but a billion two billions of us all the people of the world we will have the slogans and we will have the hymns and we will have the guns and we will use them and we will live. Make no mistake of it we will live. We will be alive and we will walk and talk and eat and sing and laugh and feel and love and bear our children in tranquility in security in decency in peace. You plan the wars you masters of men plan the wars and point the way and we will point the gun."

I have to pause sometimes reading when my voice cracks from emotion. I say, "It doesn't have to be outrage. It can be beauty." I read a description by Terry Tempest Williams, the opening strains from *Desert Quartet:* "Earth. Rock. Desert. I am walking barefoot on sandstone, flesh responding to flesh. It is hot, so hot the rock threatens to burn through the calloused soles of my feet. I must quicken my pace, paying attention to where I step. For as far as I can see, the canyon country of southern Utah extends in all directions. No compass can orient me here, only a pledge to love and walk the terrifying distances before me. What I fear and desire most in this world is passion. I fear it because it promises to be spontaneous, out of my control, unnamed, beyond my reasonable self. I desire it because passion has color, like the landscape before me. It is not pale. It is not neutral. It reveals the backside of the heart. I climb the slickrock on all fours, my hands and feet throbbing with the heat. It feels good to sweat, to be engaged, to inhabit my animal body."

I read beautiful and impassioned descriptions from Susan Griffin, E. M. Forster, and yes, Stephen King.

"Nor does it have to be rock music," I say. I change CDs and play the opening bars of Beethoven's Fifth. I change again and cue

Beethoven's Ninth to the "Ode to Joy." I move again to the chalk-board. I pick up a long piece of chalk, smash it against the chalkholder to break it in two. With the long end I write, "Let the kid out of the closet." Intentionally, I press too hard, and the chalk splinters on the board. I whirl and throw what remains in my hand against the back wall. I pick up more chalk and throw it around the room, as hard as I can. Chalk explodes against every wall. I write, "Unleash the beast!" I write, "Who are you?" I write, "Have fun!" I write, "Let go!" I write, "¡No Pasaran!" I throw more chalk.

The music winds down. Sweat hangs from strands of hair that curl around my face. I put in one final CD, and ask someone to hit the lights. The room goes dark, save the red power indicator on the CD player. I play "Time," by Pink Floyd:

> *Ticking away the moments that make up a*
> *dull day;*
> *Fritter and waste the hours in an off hand*
> *way.*
> *Kicking around on a piece of ground in your*
> *home town;*
> *Waiting for someone or something to show*
> *you the way.*
> *Tired of lying in the sunshine, staying home*
> *to watch the rain,*
> *You are young and life is long, and there is*
> *time to kill today.*
> *And then one day, you find ten years have*
> *got behind you.*
> *No one told you when to run. You missed*
> *the starting gun.*
> *Run and you run to catch up with the sun,*
> *but it's sinking;*

Racing around to come up behind you again.

The sun is the same in the relative way, but you're older,

Shorter of breath, and one day closer to death.

Ev'ry year is getting shorter, never seem to find the time.

Plans that either come to naught, or half a page of scribbled lines.

Hanging on in quiet desperation is the English way.

The time is gone. The song is over, thought I'd something more to say.

We sit in the dark a few moments. No one says anything. Finally someone turns on the lights. I say, "I think that's enough for one day. Have a great evening."

~

It's the next class period. I begin by saying, "I'd like for you now to do the most important writing exercise there is. It's a finger exercise. Writing is hard work, and just like in track or any other sport, you have to stretch before you work out or you could pull a muscle. But even before you stretch you have to warm up a little bit. So, everybody shake out your hands."

They stare.

"For real. Shake 'em up."

They put their hands in front of them and shake.

"Now, hold your hands up, palms facing you."

They do it.

"The first thing is to reach with your thumb all the way over to the pad of your pinky. Stretch, stretch, stretch. Now, fold your pinky to cover your thumbnail. With me? Next, stretch down your first finger to cover the base knuckle of your thumb. That's a hard one. Finally, take your ring finger and cover your thumb's middle knuckle."

It takes a moment for them to catch up.

I say, "That's the most important writing exercise you can ever do. Do it often, at all authority figures, and especially at your internal critic."

They laugh.

They still don't know I'm serious.

The function of high school, then, is not so much to communicate knowledge as to oblige children finally to accept the grading system as a measure of their inner excellence. And a function of the self-destructive process in American children is to make them willing to accept not their own, but a variety of other standards, like a grading system, for measuring themselves. It is thus apparent that the way American culture is now integrated it would fall apart if it did not engender feelings of inferiority and worthlessness.

—Jules Henry

grades

As I've written elsewhere, grades are a problem. On the most general level, they're an explicit acknowledgment that what you're doing is insufficiently interesting or rewarding for you to do it on your own. Nobody ever gave you a grade for learning how to play, how to ride a bicycle, or how to kiss. One of the best ways to destroy love for any of these activities would be through the use of grades, and the coercion and judgment they represent. Grades are a cudgel to bludgeon the unwilling into doing what they don't want to do, an important instrument in inculcating children into a lifelong pattern of subservience to whatever authority happens to be thrust over them.

More specifically as it relates to writing, it struck me immediately as absurd, immoral, and counterproductive to ask people to write from the heart, and then give them grades: "This is an extraordinarily courageous retelling of the long-term effects of your childhood sexual abuse by your father, starkly told. I have to say, however, that not only is this paper a week late but that your organization is lacking, and several times you've misspelled *trauma*. You forgot the *u*. You get a C–."

I also recognize, though, that there are times when some form of external motivation or accountability can be helpful. When I was first teaching myself how to write, in my mid to late twenties, writing wasn't very fun. Someone had told me, you're not a real writer until you've written a million words, so nerd that I am, I started keeping track of how many words I wrote. Since I also knew, as another writer had told me, that writing is rewriting, and because I *really was* a nerd, I created a system where every word I wrote in the first draft of a story or article counted as one

71

word, every word in the second draft counted as half a word, those in the third draft a third of a word, and so on. I set myself a goal of a thousand words a day. At that rate I would be a writer, so the plan went, in a little under three years. I wasn't able to meet that daily goal (miss only one day at a thousand words, and you've got to write two thousand the next!), but I was able to average about five hundred. I had to force myself to do it. It was hard, unpleasant work. The problem was that I was writing only with my head. I hadn't yet found my heart, hadn't been able to find that door that opens to the places where the muse lives, the door to other worlds or to this one. For that matter, I hadn't been able to find the door that opens to where *I* live. And so everything was work.

I once read an interview with a writer who was asked, "Does the writing ever get easier?"

The writer's answer: "No, but it gets better."

For me, writing has gotten much easier. If writing were as hard for me today as it was fifteen years ago, I wouldn't be writing. Life is way too short to work that hard at something that feels so uncomfortable. Part of the earlier sensation of difficulty and discomfort for me, though, wasn't the writing itself. It was frustration because my skills didn't match my reach. In other words, when writing felt difficult, which most of the time it did, it was almost always because I didn't have the skills, information, or perspective to be able to accurately and adequately convey whatever I was trying to communicate. That still happens, but nowadays I don't try to force it. I got stuck yesterday after the fourth sentence of this paragraph, and instead of getting frustrated staring at the computer screen I just did other things until late last night when the next sentence came to me.

I no longer think getting stuck is a bad thing. No longer does it frustrate me. Now, it just gives me information. The information could be that I don't yet know enough about the subject, and need to do more research. There's not much that's harder than describing a beach if you've never been to one. There's not much that's easier if you have. The same is true not just for descriptions of places but for arguments as well: One of the great joys of my life is that I get to bump up against questions I don't understand, and attempt to feel my way through them. Writing at first bump remains difficult, if not impossible. But having taken the time to settle all the way into the question, and to let it reveal as much of itself as it cares to, writing becomes relatively easy as I lay out the questions, answers, and, when appropriate, the processes in between as clearly and interestingly as possible. For example, early in my book *The Culture of Make Believe*, I spent a couple of very fun weeks researching and ruminating on the precise relationship between hatred, contempt, entitlement, and threats to that entitlement before the answer came clear, partly through a quote I stumbled upon by Nietzsche, "One does not hate when one can despise." So long as entitlement can be maintained through tradition, philosophy, economics, the school system, and so on, those in power merely feel contempt for those they exploit. But threaten that entitlement, and watch the lynchings begin. We could probably see the same thing on a much smaller scale in the classroom. So long as students defer at all times to teachers, everyone gets along fine. But if students begin to question the teachers' (or administrators') authority too seriously, the smile on the face of this form of social control starts to become a tad brittle.

Sometimes getting stuck doesn't mean I lack knowledge about the subject. It means I'm asking the wrong question. I sat stuck for a year and a half before writing a single word on my book *A Language Older Than Words* as I struggled with the question, how do I convincingly talk about the sentience and communication abilities of nonhumans? It was only when the question shifted—first to, why are some humans able and willing to listen to non-humans (and other humans), and some are not? and then further to, what is the necessary relationship between silencing and exploitation?—that I was able to write the book. Similarly, I would probably get stuck were I to attempt to write on the question, how do we make industrial civilization sustainable? Shift the question to, why/how is civilization inherently unsustainable, and what are we going to do about it? and I'll write as one possessed. Of course the questions need not be philosophical; in a novel they might be associated with a plot. For all I know, when Margaret Mitchell was writing *Gone With The Wind,* she may have gotten stuck on the question, how do I get Scarlett and Ashley out of their romantic entanglement? and was only able to proceed when she changed the question to, what sort of a relationship should Scarlett and Ashley have? (Or perhaps more accurately, what sort of a relationship does Scarlett have with herself? since I'm not sure Scarlett ever does enter into a real relationship with anyone else.)

Along these same lines, sometimes getting stuck means I've taken a wrong turn. I often liken writing to being a dog following a scent. Sometimes I lose the scent. Then I back up a sentence. Is this where I got lost? Then I back up another, and another, until I find the place where I no longer feel lost but as though I've once again found the scent. Then I can proceed.

Other times it doesn't so much mean I've taken a wrong turn as it means I'm writing a piece I really don't want to write. It's very difficult to force myself to write something I don't want to (or to do something I don't want to), and it gets more difficult as I grow older (with that much less time to waste before I die), and as I become more comfortable within myself. I'm not the first to remark that the sensation of work (in its unpleasant sense) often arises as a result of friction between different parts of the self. When different parts of the self act in alignment, the "work" is more or less frictionless. Anyone who has entered "the zone" in athletics has experienced this. The same is true for writing, for relationships, for all of life. I've sometimes taken to saying, "most of my decisions are wrong," because usually when I'm heading in the right direction there are no decisions to be made. Certainly there are vital exceptions to this: I've been in situations where I should have left—bad jobs, bad relationships—and the lack-of decision was to stay. It took a decisive act to leave, but note that these situations were never frictionless in the first place.

At still other times getting stuck means I'm not yet ready to write the piece. I wrote the first ten pages of this book a couple of years ago, found I'd lost the scent, backed up, couldn't find it, and decided the book needed to not be written right then. I wrote another book instead. Then I returned to this book a few weeks ago, backed up one sentence, and found the scent was now clean, the book ready to be written. Had I written it two years ago, it would have been a different book, one that was not very fun to write and probably not very good.

All of which is to say that in the last fifteen years one of the few things I've learned is how to tell when I'm writing crap—the writing doesn't flow, it's frustrating, and I'm writing with my head, not my body—and to not write it. ("Doctor, doctor, it hurts when I do this." "Well, don't do that.")

If I may be allowed to switch similes, I also sometimes liken writing to fishing. I can't take out a club, start beating the water, and expect to catch many fish. So I can't be too aggressive, try to force the writing. But neither will I catch fish if I don't have my line in the water. So I can't be too passive. I need to always be attending to the work. When I got stuck yesterday and did other things, I kept returning in my mind to the place where I was stuck to see if there was any movement, any sign of what I should do next.

All of this is true, I believe, not just of writing, but of many things.

It's something of a paradox. On one hand, everything I've written in the past few pages militates against external schedules or motivations, and, as it relates to the discussion of teaching writing (or, for that matter, teaching anything), against grades. On the other hand, I'm fully aware that had I never set myself an entirely artificial goal of writing a thousand words a day, I never would have made it through the painful and difficult process of learning how easy writing can be. The same was true on a slightly smaller scale for the writing of *A Language Older Than Words*. Having gotten tired of sitting on a book that wasn't being written, I told myself that if I didn't start it within the next three months I would drop the project entirely and move on to something else. Two weeks before the deadline the operant question shifted, and then a week later it shifted again. The book got written in the next year.

I've also lived long enough on the steep parts of enough different learning curves to know that writing is by no means unique in its requirement of a difficult apprenticeship before things get easier. I've experienced that in science, beekeeping, basketball, high jumping, interpersonal communication, interspecies communication, listening to dreams, figuring out what I want to do with my life. You name it.

There's still a difference, though, between what I've been writing about in these past few pages, and grades. Don't let me sneak that difference by you. The goals and deadlines I set, artificial though they may have been, were still set by me. They weren't imposed from the outside by authority figures who thought they knew my processes better than I, as is typical in the classroom. Nor were they set by outsiders to whom I gladly defer because of their expertise and experience. For example, whenever I used to go hunting, I always deferred to both of my hunting partners, because they were far better and more experienced hunters than I. I remember that once, as I rode with Johnny along a rough dirt road through scablands, he suddenly took one of his hands off the steering wheel, pointed, and said, "I hate it when they do that." I followed his gaze and saw a crow sitting with its head just above the grass. Johnny stopped the truck. We got out, and walked to where he'd pointed. We saw the bodies of a doe and her fawn. They'd been poached. Even driving, Johnny had seen one ear sticking above the grass, and a few feet away a crow standing taller than it should have—perched on the head of the fawn—and from that had filled in the scene. I'd seen nothing more than the head of a black bird off to the side, and had thought nothing of it at all. You can see why I deferred. But had my partners shown themselves unworthy of my respect I would have withdrawn my deference. Now, I did have more writing experience than my students (I, after all, had written—and counted—my million words), but their deference was never optional. And while I certainly have had my share of teachers— inside classrooms and out—who have deserved my respect, and whom I've allowed and even encouraged to set goals or deadlines for me, I've also had my share who've not deserved that respect. Yet in classrooms I was expected to defer to them, to do tasks they assigned me, and to accept judgments they pronounced on those tasks and on me, no matter the teachers' bigotry, ignorance, arrogance, or narcissism (I'm not suggesting, by the way, that teachers are more bigoted, ignorant, arrogant, or narcissistic than anyone else, but, and this is the point, nor are they less). It's an impossible situation. As a student who cares about your soul, or as a teacher who cares about the souls of your students (as well as, for that matter, your own), what are you going to do?

Just tonight I received an e-mail from an acquaintance on exactly this subject. She wrote, "I went into teaching wanting to do it differently, to be the kind of teacher who leads by example, not by coercion. But once I get into the daily grind of the work that I do, surrounded by people who insist that I support the status quo—administrators, other teachers, parents, students—I start to slide. I start to forget why I'm there and what I'm trying to do. Instead my goal becomes to get through the day without getting criticized. I get worn down. And I start to hate my job because I'm constantly trying to use power I don't believe in to enforce policies I don't believe in. And I'm feeling so pressured and stressed and busy that I don't even realize that is what's going on, until it gets so bad that it forces me to stop and spend time reevaluating. Then I recommit to working for change, but the second I get back in that environment, the slow erosion begins again. It reminds me of a poem by a local poet, whom I recommend highly. Her name is Claudio Mauro. 'You wouldn't think / It would be so easy / To forget / Who we really are / Or that death is always at our shoulder / Or that everything is alive / Or that God is everywhere singing.'"

~

"If thinking about making your writing better than sex doesn't work for you," I say, "here's another way to think about it. Charles Johnson—the writer, not the catcher—said something about this in an interview. I read them the following paragraph: "I think a real writer simply has to think in other terms. Not, 'Will I get in this magazine? Will I get this NEA next year?' but whether or not this work is something he would do if a gun was held to his head and somebody was going to pull the trigger as soon as the last word of the last paragraph of the last page was finished. Now if you can write out of the sense that you're going to die as soon as the work is done, then you will write with urgency, honesty, courage, and without flinching at all, as if this were the last testament in language, the last utterance you could ever make to anybody. If a work is written like that, then I want to read it. If somebody's writing out of that sense, then I'll say, 'This is serious. This person is not fooling around. This work is not a means to some other end, the work is not just intended for some silly superficial goal, this work is the writer saying something because he or she feels that if it isn't said, it will never be said.' Those are the writers I want to read. And there are not many twentieth-century writers like that."

The students are silent for a moment, until one says, "Somebody puts a gun to my head, and says they're going to kill me when I write the last word, I'm telling you right now I'm going to write a long-ass paper."

~

I tried to have my students edit each other's papers, but I gave up on that as a near-immediate disaster. They had no idea how to do it. This is not surprising. Not many people do. Editing, I learned quickly, is a skill as difficult to learn as writing, beekeeping, auto mechanics, or gardening. But even moreso it's an attitude of unselfishness, empathy, and sympathy (not only for the author but for the piece itself) that is rare within our culture.

When I went to graduate school, I took a fair number of writing workshops. They were generally awful. A writer would make copies of a story and pass them around to the people in class. The other students would ostensibly read the stories, and then come back the week after to take potshots at them. Sometimes they gave compliments as well, but even these were often not helpful, because the students had never been taught how to help. The image that kept coming to mind as my or someone else's story was getting "workshopped"—politespeak for torn apart—is that of a body on a table, with a dozen experts poking at it. Now, the body might be dead, have a sharp pain between the third and fourth ribs, or have a slight hamstring pull. The body might be full of cancer, or in perfect health. Meanwhile, each of the experts makes a diagnosis that has much more to do with that expert's preconceptions than the body at hand. The oncologist sees cancer everywhere, while the podiatrist traces it all to the feet. The acupuncturist sees energy breaks along meridians, the chiropractor sees a spine out of alignment. The voodoo specialist sees it in terms of voodoo practices. Unfortunately, none of these particular practitioners sees the actual body, for the instructors did not teach us how to see. Nor, and this is the real point, did they teach us to care about other writers. This is all damaging.

I did have two good experiences in workshops. Once, a visiting writer edited pieces written by me and one other person. He was the only person who spoke that day, and I remember he prefaced all of his suggestions with comments like, "Your instincts are right on with this bit of dialog. It sounds just like people talk. The problem is that although we tell ourselves we want our dialog to be 'realistic,' we don't. Let's see how this sounds if we try this. . . ." I learned more that day about how to write than in almost all of my other workshops combined. The other time a workshop worked, it was because, oddly enough, the instructor was ill for the first six weeks of class, so we, the students, ran the class ourselves. I don't know if the fact that we were suddenly thrust into these circumstances caused us to take care of each other, or if there is another explanation for why it worked, but it did: We somehow coalesced into a group of friends working together to try to solve specific problems that each of us would bring to the room.

The positive experiences I've had with editors have nearly always had more to do with how well the editor reads me and responds to what I'm trying to say than with the editor's technical abilities. Years ago I had a friend who did not finish high school, and rarely read, but who had the ability unerringly to locate the parts of stories that didn't yet work, and to help me fix them. She did this by reading my voice as I read the work aloud, and sensing the slightest hesitations, or noticing that I sped up at certain parts, as though I were trying to hurry past a paragraph I knew on some level was boring. I have a friend now who's even better at mirroring back to me my concerns about my pieces, who combines this exquisite sensitivity with a long history of reading, writing, and editing. These friends have taught me how to edit, and how to write.

The trick to editing, which my students had not yet learned—and this is also true of the giving of advice, and perhaps it's true of all of life—is to find out where the other person's heart resides, and then to help him or her get there.

My analysis of coercion in schooling was all very nice, but the department required I give grades. If I didn't give grades, I wouldn't be allowed to teach. (That's one advantage of teaching in prison: I don't have to give grades.) I didn't know what to do about grading students at the university. I did know I wouldn't judge my students' writing, and I also knew I needed to involve at least my first students in the process of figuring out how to assign grades. I briefly describe this process in *A Language Older Than Words*. One student suggested I give everyone a 4.0. I took this idea to my supervisor, who nixed it out of hand. I then suggested to my students that we assign grades randomly. I was surprised that not even the less-motivated students—at least some of whom would surely have benefited grade-wise—liked this idea. Even they seemed to feel that grades should correspond roughly with effort. Then I suggested I give everyone a grade of pi, or 3.14159. Math majors liked this idea, at least theoretically, but neither the administrators nor the rest of the students got the joke.

Soon enough we came to the idea of basing grades on check marks. Because you learn to write by writing, the more writing a student did, the better grade that person would get. For every paper a student wrote, the student would receive one check mark. And because writing *is* rewriting, for rewriting this paper the student would receive another check mark. These check marks would convert directly to grade points: If someone wrote one paper for each of the twelve weeks of class, and rewrote two-thirds of the papers after I had looked them over (and praised them), that person would get twelve plus eight check marks, for a grade of 2.0 on a scale of 4 (C stands for Credit!). So far, so good.

We tweaked it pretty quickly, and in so doing solved another problem. Because every student's strengths and weaknesses are particular to that student, I had wondered how I'd individually help students enhance these strengths and overcome (or sidestep) these weaknesses in the context of a classroom. One student may have a good sense of action but a poor enough grasp of grammar to leave readers wondering what the hell this writer was trying to say, and may benefit from lessons on subject and verb agreement and clear use of commas. This lesson would bore the rest of the students out of their skulls: There's almost no way you can make a grammar lecture more interesting than sex, especially for those who already understand the joys of semicolons.

Here's the solution. I said to them, "If there's a paper you especially like, you and I can cover it line by line, work on it to make the piece really sparkle. We'll conference on it again and again, and edit it until you and I are happy with every word." Even though the emphasis was on trying to finish the paper for its own sake, as opposed to strictly for the grade, for each paper they took to doneness they would get four check marks. I urged them to pursue this, and told them it would be through that process that they would really learn how to write. Most importantly, I told them, it would be fun.

It would mean I'd spend a lot of time conferencing, but that was okay; delivering encouragement and lessons about writing in private would free up class time to talk about more important things, like love.

Modern schools and universities push students into habits of depersonalized learning, alienation from nature and sexuality, obedience to hierarchy, fear of authority, self-objectification, and chilling competitiveness. These character traits are the essence of the twisted personality-type of modern industrialism. They are precisely the character traits needed to maintain a social system that is utterly out of touch with nature, sexuality, and real human needs.

—Arthur Evans

love

"Close your eyes," I say.

They stare at me.

"For real. Close them."

They do.

"Picture this. Next spring you go to a conference. It's near Atlanta. Peach blossoms are just popping. You can smell them everywhere. The conference has to do with whatever is closest to your heart. If you love physical therapy, it's a conference of physical therapists. If you love baseball, that's the subject. If you're a Christian, it's a Christian gathering. For me, it would be a bunch of people who want to bring down industrial civilization.

"You get there on a Friday, and the first lectures are Friday night. You sit near the back, but in a seat with a good view. You're very interested in the talks. There's an empty seat next to you. About ten minutes before the thing starts, you see out of the corner of your eye someone of your preferred gender approaching you. The person has to pass by you to get to the seat, and asks if anyone is sitting there. You start to stand to let the person by, but one look at that face and your knees buckle. You try again, and eventually are able to more or less stand. The person asks again, 'Is anyone sitting there?'

"You stammer, 'I hope you are.' You can't believe you just said that. But there it is.

"The person sits. You make pleasant talk before the lecture, and you're consistently impressed with the other's knowledge, humor, quick intelligence, easy vocabulary (don't large vocabularies—not pedantic ones, but naturally big ones—just make you melt?), confidence, and of course those eyes. The lecture starts. For some reason you can't focus on it, but instead you focus on the slightest shifts in the seat next to yours. Your hand brushes the other's at one point, and your heart stops."

I stop, take a deep breath. The students' eyes are still closed. Most students are smiling.

"There are some things you have to take care of after the talk, so you say, attempting, not very successfully, to sound casual, "What are you doing in an hour?"

"The person responds, 'Waiting for your phone call.'

"You call. You take a walk. You talk till three. You go to your separate rooms, and you sleep. The next day you attend the lectures, but you don't pay much attention. You talk and talk. You stay up that night again till three talking, then go to your separate rooms. Sunday you don't even bother to go to the lectures, but instead go out to the battlefield park at Kennesaw Mountain, and walk through the fields where 140 years ago men fought and died. You talk of mortality, and you talk of beauty. Late in the day, as the sun grows fat near the horizon, the person says to you, 'I know you have to go back to Spokane tomorrow, but tonight I want to spend the night with you. We've been making love these past two days by talking, and I want for our bodies to join the conversation.'"

I stop again, then say to my students, "So, the question I have for you is, what do you do?"

They open their eyes. Someone asks, "Am I in a relationship back at home?"

"For now, we'll say no."

They start to talk. Their eyes are alive. They're split fifty-fifty as to whether they would say yes or no. The same ratio of women as men say yes. One woman says, "I wouldn't have waited till the third night. Why waste the first two?"

Another says, "Why did he have to ruin it by bringing up sex?"

A third: "How would sex ruin it?"

A man says, "I'm from Japan, so of course I would say yes."

We all laugh, but don't know what this means. He tries to explain, but his English and our Japanese aren't up to it, and even he ends up laughing.

One woman says, "Not without a ring."

Some argue with her. Others (some men, some women) agree with her. I'm overjoyed—this is not hyperbole—at the lack of double standards: there is not the slightest hint of calling men wimps if they say no or women sluts if they say yes.

There are three people who seem uncomfortable with the discussion. One is a fundamentalist Christian woman who soon writes me a scathing note telling me that some things should not be talked about in class. I write her back that I agree, and vow never to talk about grammar, nor anything else boring. The other two are more interesting to me. They're a twenty-year-old man and woman who've been dating about a month. Everyone else in the room talks freely, but each time before either of them speak I see them measuring their words for potential effect on the other. I can tell that he, especially, wants to say that yes he would sleep with her in this fantasy but is afraid that if he does he may end up sleeping alone in the real world. Everyone in class picks up on their discomfort, and someone suggests teasingly that first one and then the other leave the room while the remaining one says what he or she really feels. Finally his eyes brighten as he sees a way out. He says, in a voice ostensibly directed at the class but with a message we all know is intended for her, "I know when we started this relationship, we went slower than that, but that was because we didn't want to rush a good thing. I think, though, that if we'd met at a conference like this, I'd have been all over you the first night."

He looks at her. Her face reveals nothing.

He continues, "That's not to say I would move that fast with anyone else, because I wouldn't, but with you. . . ."

She smiles, and he can breathe again.

Someone asks what I would do. I say, "In my twenties I would have been too scared, and I would have said no because of that fear. Now, I hope I would say yes, or really, I hope I'd say whatever feels right and true at the time."

No matter whether anyone says yes or no I always ask why. I ask them what's the relationship, if any, between intellectual and emotional intimacy, and between either of these and physical intimacy. It's clear I don't care what their answers are, I'm just interested in how they come to their answers.

At last I say, "Now, let's start changing the framing conditions. What if, instead, you were in a relationship back home that was on its last legs, and was never very good in the first place. Would that change how you act?"

A woman says, "I'd tell the guy I'd love to spend the night with him, but I have to make a quick phone call first."

Those who said no would still say no, obviously. Many of those who said yes would still say yes.

"Okay," I say, "what if you thought the relationship at home was good, but this one is magic. Would that change things?"

Someone says you can't call a weekend a relationship. Nothing happens that fast.

I tell him about my mother's cousin. He was in an army hospital in World War II, having been shot in the knee getting off a troop transport making an assault on an island in the Pacific. He was in the lunch room one day, and one of the nurses walked in, took one look at him, and said to the nurse standing next to her, "That's the man I'm going to marry." They've been together now almost sixty years.

Another student asks, "Why can't we just allow this wonderful weekend to be a wonderful weekend? Who's to say that's not a relationship, and just as valid and important as something that goes on for years? Why aren't people ever happy in the moment?"

I tell them of a comic strip I once saw, consisting of two identical panels of a woman sitting up in bed frowning. The caption on the left says she's contemplating a one-night stand that should have been a long-term relationship. The caption on the right says she's contemplating a long-term relationship that should have been a one-night stand.

A woman says, "The trick is to figure out which is which before there's too much regret."

The students are engaged. They seem happy. Everyone talks. I change the conditions again and again. What if you had wonderful conversations but the person wasn't so attractive as I suggested? Not Quasimodo, but pretty darn close. Would that matter? Or what if the person was physically beautiful, but you quickly discovered you had nothing to talk about? ("For example," I say, "You find out that the person likes the Three Stooges." "Hey," a guy responds, "*I* like the Three Stooges." "Well, then," I retort, "don't ask me to sleep with you.") What if instead of being 3000 miles from home you were 50 miles? What if we combine this exercise with the previous one, and you only have a limited amount of time to live? Would any of those change your actions?

Class is over. It's time to go. No one wants to leave, except the distraught fundamentalist. She packs her things and stomps out. We all stay a bit longer. People drift away.

Over the next few days I receive several phone calls from people asking if it's too late to add the class. My students returned to their dorms and talked to their roommates about these questions. The roommates talked to others down the hall, who called friends in other dorms, who got together and talked late into the night. They're excited.

The next class period, the same student who asked before what the point was of the discussion about having a fatal disease asks again what the point is here. This time I shrug and smile. I don't tell them this, but the point of the discussion was never sex. Not in the slightest. The point was to learn how to think, how to make distinctions (when would you, and when would you not?), and how to support positions (why would or wouldn't you?). The discussion was about following decision trees. But even that wasn't really the point. The point was to help them remember, after so many years of stultifying experiences in school, that thinking can and should be fun.

~

The other day we had a party at the prison. It was some of the most fun I've had in a long time. It was an editing party. Two of the students were new. The rest were old hands, having been in the class for between six months and three years. It's been a joy to watch them learn how to edit. We were working on a couple of the old hands' stories. Both of the stories are excellent, tightly plotted and energetically written. One is about a man whose addiction to crank costs him his wife, who kills herself; his daughter, who gets killed; and his freedom, as he ends up in prison. The other is about a little girl, unhappy because her parents often fight, who goes to her favorite spot on a deserted beach, falls asleep, as she often does, and awakens to see a frog boy: a boy who has been turned into a frog. They become friends. But then the scientists who shot him with a potion that turned him into a frog turn her into a dragonfly. I can't tell you what happens after that because he hasn't finished the story, but I do know that these events bring her parents back together.

We'd made copies of the pages to edit, and passed them around. We'd already heard these pages a few times, and given general comments to the authors. Now it was time to dive in. I read aloud, slowly, pausing after each sentence to see if anyone had any concerns. We came to the scene where the man shoots crank. I said, "You've described it well, but I don't yet feel it. I loved how earlier you showed the love between him and his wife. Can you help me understand why the crank feels so good he'd give up his family?"

"I have to tell you," he said, "that when I wrote this I held back, because I didn't want for someone reading it to have a relapse."

"That's death," I said. "You can't think about your audience that way and expect the writing to be as good as yours usually is. The one question I ask myself with every sentence I write is: Is this sentence true? That's the only thing that matters, and the only thing I can think about."

Another student said, "I wanted more detail. What does the room where he shoots up look like?"

And another, "Remember in Sickness's story [Sickness is another of my students] about the ex-addict, the scene where he sees his son start to eat cereal with a bent spoon, and the father has to rebend it because he doesn't want his son to be associated with drugs? Could you put in details like that?"

I said, "You describe the feeling when he shoots up as orgasmic. Is that really what it feels like. And do you feel it in your genitals?"

"My God," the author said, "I'd usually come as soon as I took the shot."

"For real?" I ask.

"Sometimes," he continued, "I'd have to sit on the toilet because I'd piss and shit and come all over."

"That's a good thing?"

Another student said, "I've heard about people doing that."

"Slow down," I said. "Tell us what happens."

He told us, in slow detail, how the whole process of shooting up works, from the moment of deciding to buy, to the purchase, to preparing the gear, to shooting up, to the rush, to coming down, and then realizing once again he'd spent his family's grocery money (someone dissuaded him from saying he'd lost the money his baby needed for new shoes).

Over and over I'd say, "That's a great detail! You're telling us now, but that's not in the story! Put it in!"

Details in, we read it again. One of the students, a former tweaker himself, wrapped his arms around himself and said, "This gives me chills."

"That's what you want," I said. "If you're going to write about drugs, you've got to make your readers addicts for that scene. You've got to make us understand why it's so great he'd give up his family. You've got to make us want to give up *our* families. It's the same with anything else. If you're describing a little girl turning into a dragonfly, your readers have to turn into dragonflies as they read it."

We asked more questions: Do bikers really call their motorcycles steeds? Does your steed really sound like thunder when you start it up, or does it sound like cannons, or does it sound like something else? Even though the main character loves his wife, there's chemistry between him and the dealer's girlfriend: What does she look like? What's she wearing?

We worked on the other story. I read it just as slowly. The questions came from around the room. What does it feel like when the wings begin to sprout? Does it itch? In this fourth sentence here, should this be a semicolon or a comma?

"I think he should break it into two sentences," someone suggested.

"No, it's a semicolon," insisted someone else.

Meanwhile, two other students were trying to figure out how Sara was going to make it down the winding game trails with her new wings, and another was wondering what she sees during her transition from single to compound eyes.

"Is she going to be able to talk?" one asked.

Another, "What's she going to eat?"

All the old hands were talking at once. I glanced at the new students, and saw on their faces looks of confusion and, frankly, concern. Suddenly I realized how the room must look to their eyes, and I burst out laughing. Here were seven or eight "hardened criminals" talking about semicolons and such with the enthusiasm of sports fans. We were, I suddenly realized, having a creative writing party. I'm not sure what could be more fun.

~

"The first rule of editing," I say to my students at Eastern Washington University, "is that the editor is not allowed to have an ego. The author can pout as much as he or she would like. But if the editor makes a suggestion and the author doesn't like it, it cannot be a big deal. I remember once long ago sharing my work with someone I dated. She made a couple of suggestions that didn't really work. I told her why, nicely. She sighed, heavily, and said, 'If you're not going to take my advice, why did you ask for it?' I knew right then I was in for a long evening.

"Another way to put this is that the author is always the boss. Yet another way to put it is that the editor must at all times have the author's best interests at heart. If you can't do that as an editor (and really, as a friend), you need to keep your mouth shut. The editor has one and only one job: to help the author write precisely what the author wants to write in the best way possible.

The editor's job is not to try to get the author to write the piece that the editor wants the author to write. I fired a couple of agents because they tried to do that. When I work with someone on one of my pieces, I have a very good sense as to whether that person is trying to help me say what I need to say. If so, I'll listen to any advice. I won't always take it, but I'll listen. If not, I won't listen at all. Everything I've said about editors applies equally to teachers. This means, and you may not be used to hearing this, especially in school, that you're the boss. I'm here—and this is true not just of editing but of everything in the classroom, for one reason—and that is to serve you.

"We perceive the entire hierarchy in school exactly opposite to how it really is. You're not here for me, and I'm not here for my supervisor. My supervisor is here to help me, the administrators are here to help him, all the way down the line. *You* are the reason we're all here. What do you want to do?"

~

I've been told by my supervisor that the official policy for attendance to my classes at Eastern Washington University should be that any student who misses more than two (without a note from a doctor) must flunk. That seems crazy to me, yet as I mentioned above, it also seems there needs to be some consequence for those students who blow off classes for no good reason but because they're irresponsible. The solution came from a student who, after being absent one day, brought in a long note from her doctor (illegibly handwritten for authenticity), whose name happened to be Frankenstein, describing how her services were needed for some work he was doing and telling me that if I happened to go to the biology department and happened to look at the collection of human brains they happened to have there, and happened to notice that one of them is missing, not to worry about it; the brain is being put to good use.

One of the only ways I got myself through school was by never reading any of the assigned texts, and still attempting to contribute to class discussions. Otherwise it was just too dull. My proudest achievement that way was the half-hour one-on-one conference with a high school English instructor about the thirty tragedies I was supposed to have read: I'd read three. I have to say, however, now having taught for several years, that I suspect my English teacher knew exactly what was going on, but, like me later, chose to reward my creativity (I actually worked much harder to learn enough about the tragedies to be able to fake it than I would have by simply reading them) instead of punish my disobedience. Likewise, I had a friend who routinely wrote book reports for books that didn't exist. I had another, as much a nerd as me and the rest of my friends, whose history papers consisted almost entirely of detailed descriptions of "obscure" battles that never took place and intricate biographies of nonexistent generals.

Of course I want to encourage that sort of thing.

What we—my students and I—come to is that every time a student is absent, one check mark will be deducted. This check mark could then be made up with another paper, preferably one as creative as the Dr. Frankenstein excuse.

～

It's the fourth week of class. Last week the student who wrote the Frankenstein story wrote a paper expressing her disgust at seeing two women kiss in her dormitory. I was struck by the desperate urgency of her disgust. On her paper, I asked what bothered her about it. Now today, in class, she asks if I think it's disgusting for women to have sex with each other.

I say, honestly enough, that I don't often think about other people's sex lives. I'm not sure I particularly want to know those sorts of details: homosexual, heterosexual, bisexual, pansexual, you name it. But when I do think about someone else's sex life, my response is generally guided by the fact that the more I hear about and understand the complexities of different people attempting to find joy and connection in our increasingly traumatized, mechanized, and fragmented society, the less capacity I find I have to judge nonmalicious, nonviolent attempts at relating to others, with no regard whatsoever for whether I would want to participate in that behavior myself.

"But," she says, "what would your parents think and do if you told them you were gay?"

I suddenly comprehend her urgency. I say, "I have no contact with my father, so I wouldn't know about him. But out of curiosity I once asked my mother that question. She said, 'First, why would I care? There's nothing wrong with it, and even if there was, it doesn't affect me. And even if it did affect me you would still have been the same person after you told me as you were five minutes before. I loved you before, so why should I love you less after?'"

"Your mother said that?"

"Yes, you certainly can see where I get my fondness for parallel sentence structure." I thought, but didn't say, *And you're hoping someday your parents will give you that same acceptance.*

~

It is six months later. That same student has come to my office. We talk about my new classes, and hers. Then she says it: "I'm dating someone."

I check the impulse to ask, "What's her name?" Instead I just smile.

She says, "She's a woman."

"Are you happy?"

"Yes," she says. "Oh, yes."

"Then so am I."

To think deeply in our culture is to grow angry and to anger others; and if you cannot tolerate this anger, you are wasting the time you spend thinking deeply. One of the rewards of deep thought is the hot glow of anger at discovering a wrong, but if anger is taboo, thought will starve to death.

—Jules Henry

thought

I t's late in the fourth week, and time for another in-class exercise, one I call the Annoying Child. The exercise: Take a strongly-held opinion and ask yourself again and again (or better, have someone ask you) why you feel the way you do, why it is important, and so on, until you either get driven to distraction, or arrive at some of the fundamental premises on which you've built your opinion.

Here's an example. Strongly held opinion: Baseball's designated hitter rule stinks.

Question from the annoying child: Why?

Answer from the perspicacious and patient adult: The rule causes managers to sidestep difficult decisions. What do you do, for example, if it's the top of the seventh, you're down two to nothing, you've got runners on second and third with two down, the pitch count is 97, your bullpen is tired from the last few days, and your pitcher comes to the plate? Do you pinch hit in the hopes of tying the game, but then have to go to the pen, or do you keep your pitcher in and probably not score?

The child asks: Why, in this case, is sidestepping difficult questions a bad thing? (Okay, so the kid is really smart, with a great vocabulary.)

The adult answers: Difficult decisions—moral, ethical, practical, what have you—are the essence of drama. They create tension. And, at least in entertainment, tension and drama are good. Just as in a good novel or play, you want the protagonist, in this case the manager, to face difficult decisions. In *Hamlet,* the protagonist must decide whether or not to kill his stepfather. If the Cardinals play the Dodgers, Tony LaRussa must decide whether or not to pinch hit for Matt Morris.

Why is tension or drama good in entertainment?

The first five rules of writing: Don't bore the reader. Would people watch if there were no tension?

Why are managerial decisions in low-scoring games more dramatic than home runs? What could be more exciting than being down by two in the bottom of the ninth, and somebody hits a walk-off three-run homer?

For whatever reason I prefer mental challenges to physical ones. Maybe because it's more fun for me to put myself in the manager's position and agonize over decisions (and don't even *think* about asking me why I find it fun to agonize) than to put myself in the player's position and feel the rush of hitting the ball on the sweet part of the bat, then watching it carry.

If that's the case, why did you daydream in junior high about hitting home runs instead of managing baseball teams?

Even when I was a kid I preferred pitchers' duels to home run contests, so I don't think it's simply that I was more athletic then, and my fantasies ran to my proclivities. I think the difference is between doing and watching. If I'm going to watch something, whether it's a movie or a baseball game, and if I have to make a choice, I'd rather be stimulated by intellectual drama than action. That's certainly true for me with books and movies, although I like it best of all when the story includes both. And it does seem that the designated hitter rule at least to some extent *forces* that choice, providing action at the direct expense of difficult decisions.

The point of this exercise—and it's useful to keep it going as long as you can stand it—is to help you flesh out your prejudices. Just as you want to take your readers with you as your main character saunters, shuffles, or sneaks into a room (maybe a dark room, with a little bit of light, that holds a musical instrument), and a primary way to do this is to describe precisely what your main character sees, hears, tastes, touches, and smells, so too, you want to take your readers with you as you make an argument, and so you describe your positions as precisely and fundamentally as possible, making clear, insofar as you can, your own biases (such as my bias toward decision-based drama over action). But the primary purpose is not really to help readers: It's to help the writer learn how to think more clearly, and not to be a slave to his or her own unquestioned assumptions.

I do this exercise all the time with my own writing, and with as many of my strongly held opinions as I can. For example, here's a strong opinion I've written about a lot: Industrial civilization can never be sustainable.

Why do you say that?

No way of living based on the use of nonrenewable resources, or the hyperexploitation of renewable resources, can ever be sustainable.

Why is that?

If your way of life is based on your use of something that exists in finite quantities (for example, oil), eventually you'll use it up. When you do, where will you be? Similarly, if your way of life is based on your use of something that renews itself, though not so quickly as you use it, eventually you'll use that up as well.

Why do you care?

Because I care about those who'll come later who'll inherit a ravaged world, and because I care about the world that is being ravaged.

Why do you care about them?

Because I'm human.

Why does being human imply you should care?

Because a human being is not simply an ego structure in a sack of skin. Human beings, and this is true for all beings, are the relationships they share. My health—emotional, physical, moral—is inextricably intertwined with the quality of these relationships, whether I acknowledge the relationships or not. If the relationships are impoverished, or if I systematically eradicate those beings with whom I pretend I do not have relationships, I am so much smaller, so much weaker. These statements are as true physically as they are emotionally and spiritually.

I ask a student to give an opinion. She says, "We need wild salmon."

"Why?"

She's fast: "Diversity is strength."

"Why is that important?

"Wild communities with the most diversity are the most stable. If there is some disaster, they're more able to recover."

"Why do you care about that?"

She thought, then came back with, "The strength that diversity gives is not only to the physical world, but also to the mental and emotional world. Everything has a lesson for our human communities, not in any woo-woo way of talking fish but in the way we have always learned how to live in a particular place. Observing and cooperating with everything around us has been the basis of our species' evolution and our personal development. More diverse habitat means more lessons, which means more chance of our own survival within that particular habitat."

"Why do we need *these* salmon? Why can't we just farm them?"

"We could farm all the salmon we need to eat, but with all our technical cleverness, we would still not know how to live here. The salmon teach us about more than themselves. If we observe wild salmon and their reactions to our actions, we will learn about clean drinking water, food-bearing trees, respect for our upstream and downstream neighbors. If we objectify salmon as meat and isolate them—ignore their lessons—we can continue our actions, destroy everything, and then die. The same is true for all the diversity around us. If we ignore all the big and small lessons around us (and limit our neighbors to only those who can live in the conditions we create) we are free to destroy whatever we want and die even sooner."

The class is stunned. So am I. Her analysis is brilliant.

I break the students into pairs, and ask them to practice this asking. The point, I stress, is not for them to turn into so many Perry Masons tearing apart each other's arguments, but to gently find with them their contradictions and weak points, then help them enlarge their thinking to encompass the contradictions and hone their thinking to pare away the weaknesses.

The real point, as always, is to have fun.

~

We finish the exercise. It's time to go. By now I'm conferencing at least an hour before and after each class. Tonight my final conference is with the woman who didn't like our classroom conversation about sex. I walk the previous student to the door of my office, then stand aside while the woman comes in. She moves directly, unhesitatingly, to my chair, and sits in it. No student has ever done this before. I pause a moment, then simply sit in the other chair. It doesn't roll, but I don't think I'll be going anywhere anyway.

She cuts to the chase: "You're in danger, and you're dangerous to the people in your classes."

I'm not sure what to say.

She continues, "You're going to hell, and if you don't stop, you'll bring a lot of people with you."

"I don't understand."

"Don't you realize what you're doing?"

I shake my head. I start to wonder if she has a gun.

"Where does faith fit into a world where people think for themselves?"

"Why do you say," I ask, "that critical thought destroys faith?"

She slides off her chair to kneel in front of me. She puts one hand on her heart, and one hand on my knee. If my chair had rollers, I'd wheel it backwards. She bows her head.

"Are you sure . . ." I start, but before I can finish she begins to pray.

She asks God to forgive me, and asks Him to help me see the danger I'm in.

Her backpack is on the floor behind her. I look over her shoulder to see if the pack's zipper is open or shut. It's open. I'll watch for quick movements. I'm glad she's touching my knee: That way I can feel sudden shifts in posture before they happen. I wish another student—any other student—waited outside.

But there's another part of me that immediately wonders who this woman really is. I wonder what she wants from me—not superficially, but deep beneath her fears—and how I can help her get to wherever it is she wants to go.

The woman continues to pray, begging God to help me understand.

I'd like to say, writing this many years later, that suddenly I understood, that I was able to see her point and change my ways, if that is what was called for, or at least that I was able to see through what she said to what she really meant and wanted, as I was able to do for the woman disgusted by seeing two women kiss. Basically, I wish I could say that I was able to help either myself or her. But neither happened. She calmly prayed over me, then got back into her chair (or rather my chair)—we talked a while longer (or rather she talked a while longer)—and then she left.

I talked to my supervisor about her, and he said that he would be happy to move her to another section if I thought that would help. I thanked him, then said I'd wait a day or two and see what happened.

She showed up an hour before the next class, and apologized. Her behavior, she said, had been entirely unacceptable, and she would drop the class if that was what I wanted. I told her not to worry about it, that everything would be fine.

I'd like to say, finally, that her apology had been the result of some sort of epiphany, whether I had anything to do with it or not, and that she participated in, and enjoyed, the rest of the class. Or maybe I'd rather say she had an epiphany that caused her to dislike the class even more: That, too, would have made me happy, so long as it involved her becoming more herself. But the truth, so far as I could tell, was neither. She continued in the class more or less disinterested, once again so far as I could tell, in everything that went on.

But that's okay, too. To demand an epiphany of any sort from students is just as coercive as to demand one specific epiphany from them. I cannot control what my students want or are able to learn, and I have no desire to. Nor can I control whether the students like the class, and I have no desire to do that either. Nor can I control whether they are at a place in their lives to learn from anything I have to offer. To attempt to control any of these would be to reproduce in my own classroom the bureaucratic model that is killing the world, a model that values standardization over individuality, preconception over presence, and what I want, or believe I want, over what the student actually needs.

It's very easy to accept and nurture students who, having been inculcated into always deferring to their teachers, defer also to my plans for them to think for themselves, or at least what I perceive as them thinking for themselves. But if my acceptance and nurturance of them is to be anything more than a velvet glove over the same old iron fist of the teacher, I must also be just as willing (and in fact just as eager) to accept them when they choose—or make no choice—to follow a path different than the one I've laid out for them. It makes no difference that I perceive myself as trying to encourage them to go down their own paths. What I perceive as the direction they need to head may bear no relationship to the direction they actually need to head, the direction they're capable of heading, or the direction they indeed end up heading. And I need at all times to defer to that uncertainty, that mystery.

But that doesn't mean I need to let them sit in my chair.

It's ironic. Radicals dream midnight police raids, or sit around over coffee and talk with glittering eyes about Repression—about those internment camps that are waiting empty. And all the time Miss Jones does her quiet thing with the kids in third grade. People like to chat about the fascist threat or the communist threat. But their visions of repression are for the most part romantic and self indulgent: massacres, machine guns drowning out La Marseillaise. And in the meantime someone stops another tenth grader for a hall-pass check and notices that his T-shirt doesn't have a pocket on it. In the meantime the Bank of America hands out another round of high-school achievement awards. In the meantime I grade another set of quizzes. God knows the real massacres continue. But the machine gun isn't really what is to be feared most in our civilized Western world. It just isn't needed all that much. The kids leave Miss Jones' class. And they go on to junior high and high school and college. And most of them will never need to be put in an internment camp. Because they're already there. Do you think I'm over-stating it? That's what's so frightening: we have the illusion that we're free. In school we learn to be good little Americans—or Frenchmen—or Russians. We learn how to take the crap that's going to be shoveled on us all our lives. In school the state wraps up people's minds so tight that it can afford to leave their bodies alone. Repression? You want to see victims of repression? Come look at most of the students at San Diego State College, where I work. They want to be told what to do. They don't know how to be free. They've given their will to this institution just as they'll continue to give their will to the institutions that engulf them in the future.

—Jerry Farber

choices

$\int$ tudents liked the check-mark system, in part because they
always knew where they stood, but moreso because they determined their own grades. Something I never liked especially about
college was that I often had no idea what grades I would get until
I received them in the mail. More than a few times I spent frantic
weekends before finals cramming for tests that could determine
whether or not I had to retake classes, then had to wait two
weeks to discover my fate. (I have to admit, though, that more
often these study sessions turned into marathon games of "calculator case baseball," where we stuffed a soft calculator case full
of papers, then used our hands as bats to play an indoor version
of over the line in an empty classroom (if the case lands anywhere
in the first three rows, you're out; next four rows, single; next
four, double; final two, triple; back wall, homer; if the case is
caught, or lands on a desk or in a chair, you're out)). And it all
seemed so capricious anyway. We've all experienced tests where
the majority of the questions come from sections we for whatever
reason studied least. And what, more than anything, do tests
really test? Our ability to take tests. What's the use—or fun—of
that? With the check-mark system there were no surprises.

That's not to say we didn't tweak the system, because we did,
often. One of the first changes was that I limited the number of
papers students could turn in per week. The average grade at
midquarter was usually about 0.7 (of course!). By the ninth of
twelve weeks it was usually about 1.7. Then panic would set in,
and I'd be handed each week huge piles of papers by students

frantic to raise their grades fast. These papers were, naturally, for the most part crap. I didn't like that, not only for my own sake, and not only because students didn't get the benefit of writing through the quarter, but also because not many people have more than two or three things to say in any given week. Most important of all, though, is that because writing is about process (as is life: What is there to life apart from the process of living?), I wanted writing and rewriting papers to be about the process of discovery and writing, not about check marks. So I said students could turn in no more than three papers per week. They were fine with this.

Next, we decided that even though it was a writing class, students should receive check marks for other forms of expression. A chef from Kuwait cooked us a seven-course traditional meal, and showed us a slideshow of his home. Someone else brought a video of himself rock climbing. Another person danced for us (there was a former stripper in one of my classes, but she wasn't the one who danced). Yet another brought an audiotape of himself playing a piano concerto. A woman played the violin. One woman, with the class's permission, brought her ten- and twelve-year-old children. A man brought fruit from his orchard and vegetables from his garden. Many people brought drawings. I encouraged students to bring between one and four of these alternative forms of expression.

We soon realized, however, that it's madness to think that all learning comes from putting pen to paper, or even from putting dough into an oven to bring cookies to your writing class. What about life itself? How do you learn from life? The best way I know is by doing things I've never done before. So we decided that every time a student did something new and then wrote up a paragraph or so on it, the student would get a check mark. This was an immediate and overwhelming success. Rock music connoisseurs went to classical concerts, and classical musicians went to minor league baseball games. Jocks went to foreign-language movies (several became Kurosawa fans because of it). A generally conservative policeman participated in an anti-fur demonstration, and got hooked on civil disobedience. I was surprised at the number of people who had reached the age of twenty having never experienced Indian food. A former Seventh-Day Adventist had her first ham and cheese sandwich. One student tried (unsuccessfully) to get credit for ordering something different at Taco Bell (had he been so rigid that this was truly something new I would have given him credit, but he was just trying to scam an extra tenth of a point). One fellow stayed up for four days and nights to see what would happen; toward the end his eyes were hollow, and he'd long-since begun to giggle at things no one else understood, or perhaps even heard. A few went on the first dates of their lives. I had to put a limit of fifteen check marks per person after one guy wrote one paper and had thirty-nine new experiences in the twelve weeks: I marveled at the extraordinary creativity he showed in coming up with so many profoundly new things (the only one I remember now is something called "forward rappelling," where you, terrifyingly enough, lower yourself off a cliff face-downward instead of facing the sky, as normal), but it was, after all, a writing class.

I still faced a slight technical problem. Imitation is a powerful, and common, learning tool. When I was a child pitching in Little League, I modeled my leg kick after Juan Marichal's, and my follow-through, unfortunately, after Bob Gibson's. Later as a high jumper I watched other jumpers—both on film and in person—to try to copy the parts of their technique I thought were improvements over mine. I've done the same in life: When I see someone who has a characteristic I like, whether it's appropriate generosity, appropriate ferocity, appropriate tenderness, or appropriate relentlessness, I've attempted to incorporate that tendency into myself. And of course this is true in art. Painters have known it forever. So have musicians ("My Sweet Lord," anyone?). And wasn't it T. S. Eliot who wrote, "Immature poets imitate; mature poets steal"? When I was teaching myself how to write I'd hand copy (longhand) entire pages from books I liked, forcing myself to slow down and pass the words through my body—from my eyes to brain into my bloodstream and through my guts and heart and lungs before I settled on which passage to copy, then moving again through eyes and brain and down my arms to come out my fingertips—thus learning how the words felt in every part of me. From this I learned what a good beginning feels like, a good ending, a good description. I learned how great writers move someone across a room, show pain, show love. Even now, before I begin a book, story, or essay, I often sit on the floor and gather fifteen or twenty books around me, then read and reread their opening lines and the lines that follow (I'm getting excited now just thinking about what books I'll choose to use as examples!): "Few books today, are forgivable." "When he was nearly thirteen, my brother Jem got his arm badly broken at the elbow." "The ordinary response to atrocities is to banish them from consciousness." "I remember my childhood names for grasses and secret flowers. I remember where a toad may live and what time the birds awaken in the summer—and what trees and seasons smelled like—how people looked and walked and smelled even." "I was twelve going on thirteen when I first saw a dead human being. It happened in 1960, a long time ago . . . although sometimes it doesn't seem that long to me. Especially on the nights I wake up from dreams where the hail falls into his open eyes." "Human development may follow one of two paths: that of *love* or that of *power*." "Civilization originates in conquest abroad and repression at home." I allow—encourage—the texture of these lines to permeate me, and through me my writing.

I hoped the same for my students. Thus the problem: how to get them to read. At first I tried asking, and not even for very much: forty pages per week, of whatever they wanted to read. I told them I preferred they vary their reading, experiment as they were doing with their foods and other entertainment. But it soon became apparent that almost no one was doing any reading at all. Not that I blamed them: Reader that I am, as an undergraduate I would probably on principle have gone on a reading strike if a teacher asked me to read (hell, I *did* go on reading strikes on principle). I asked if this was the case, and it's a testament to the trust we'd established that they told the truth. I asked another instructor how to handle this, and his suggestion dovetailed perfectly with improving their writing, so I took it. I made them copy a page by hand (once again, longhand: typing is too fast) from the materials they'd read that week. If they didn't do this they'd lose check marks. They soon found themselves enjoying this process, too, and turned these copied pages into not only a chance to take someone else's writing into their bodies, but also as another opportunity for self-expression, bringing me their favorite pages from their favorite books.

~

We all make choices. Every moment of every day. Right now, I can write this sentence, or I can write a different sentence. I can turn off the light and go to sleep. I can play a game on the computer. I can pet the dogs and cats. I can call a friend. I can get in my car (despite the fact that I've not yet chosen to fix the rear left tire, which is flat) and thump down the road to the nearest dam that's killing salmon, and I can attack it with pick and shovel. I can try to swim to Siberia, and probably die in the attempt.

Every teacher makes choices, every moment of every day. She

chooses what and how to teach, and whether to teach at all. Simply because she follows her job description, follows tradition, follows what she expects her boss wants her to do does not mean she's not making choices. Choices by default are choices nonetheless.

Every student makes choices, too, every moment of every day. He chooses what and how to learn, and whether to learn at all. Simply because he follows his job description as well, follows tradition, follows what he expects his parents, teachers, friends want him to do does not mean he's not making choices.

Every person who dropped Zyklon-B crystals into rooms of doomed Jews made a choice at that moment. Every bureaucrat who kept trains running smoothly to death camps made choices. Every American (or non-American) soldier who drops bombs on civilian (or for that matter, military) targets makes choices. Every politician or general who tells them to drop those bombs makes choices. Every person who works in factories assembling those bombs, making aluminum or fuel for the aircraft to carry the bombs, paying taxes to pay for the bombs, makes choices every second. Just today, after writing this paragraph, I received in the mail a note from the IRS telling me I have to refile my tax return for a previous year: I may owe taxes when I thought I did not. I now have a choice. I can pay the taxes and in doing so support the murder and economic exploitation of humans and nonhumans the world over, or I can not pay and see what happens. Simply because we may be punished for making certain choices does not mean we're not choosing. In fact a central way our culture moves forward is by making destructive or self-destructive options seem or be the best choice in a given situation.

Every rapist makes choices. Every child abuser makes choices. Every person who beats a romantic partner makes choices. That the way these people perceive the world may have been affected by prior violence done to them does not alter the fact that they

are making choices. The near ubiquity of these horrors—25 percent of all women in our culture are raped within their lifetimes
and another 19 percent fend off rape attempts, and 565,000
American children are killed or injured by their parents or
guardians each year—suggests a lot of people are making these
choices, which means that social framing conditions cause a lot of
people to perceive these choices as viable, in fact optimal.

Every deforester makes choices. Every engineer who designs
dams or who helps drill for oil makes choices. Every genetic engineer makes choices. That these choices are rewarded by our economic system does not make them any less choices. Nor does it
absolve those who make these choices of their responsibility for
their effects.

Every person who sells her life to a job she does not like makes
choices. That her choices may be at least partially constrained by
our economic system does not make them any less choices.

We make choices in great measure based on how we see the
world. If you see the world in a particular way, it can make some
sort of sense to sell your life to a job you do not not love.
Otherwise no one would do it. Similarly, there are lenses you can
look through that make it seem reasonable to deforest. There are
lenses through which it makes sense for child abusers to abuse,
and for rapists to rape: there are reasons these people make the
choices they do. It is possible to perceive the world such that you
choose to drop bombs on people from 30,000 feet, and it is possible to perceive the world such that you choose to pay for these
bombs. It is possible to perceive the world such that it makes
sense to gas Jews and others at death camps. It is possible to perceive yourself and others such that it makes sense to destroy the
planet in order to make money and amass power, to perpetuate
and make grow an economic system. None of this is to say these
are *wise* choices: It's to say they're choices. It's also to stress, once

again, how often unquestioned assumptions frame our choices. If we wish to make different choices we must smash the frames that constrain us. We must, if we care about our own lives, and if we care about the life of the planet, begin to remember how to think critically, how to think for ourselves.

~

The picture's caption: "Fortino Samano Moments before His Execution, 1916: Fortino Samano, a cruel and cool-headed rebel leader during the Mexican Revolution, was killed by the Federal forces in 1916. He became a famous figure because he stood before his executioners, unblindfolded, and gave them the order to fire. He was so calm that not even the long ash of his cigar hit the ground before he did." The picture: a man stands, hands in his pockets, in front of a wall. He wears a fedora. His right foot rests on a stone, his right knee is slightly bent. His face betrays no fear, only perhaps a slight defiance. His lips are parted, revealing teeth clamped casually—at least seemingly so—to a cigar.

I show my students the photograph, read them the caption. It's the fourth week. By now they've gotten pretty good at telling their own stories, and it's time for them to try seeing the world from another perspective. "I want you," I say, "to write from the perspective of someone in this story. I don't care who it is. You can be Fortino Samano. You can be a fly on the wall behind him. You can be a member of the firing squad. You can be the photographer. You can be the camera. You can be someone from the village watching the execution. You can be a dog in the street. I don't care. All I care about is that you be honest. *Be* whomever you write about. No, don't write *about* someone: write *as* someone. Any questions?"

Again, I slowly show the photograph around the room. Again and again I read them the caption. They think. They stare. Some close their eyes. With my encouragement, some stand, walk to the wall, put a pencil or pen or cigarette in their mouth, and try to put themselves bodily in Samano's place, trying to see if their bodies will tell them what to write. Others stand as members of the firing squad. Still others sit, and continue to stare. And then they begin to write.

Some have a hard time with this. They speechify a bit much, use language not immediate enough for the circumstances. They don't let themselves feel whatever it is the character would feel. Instead they describe the feelings from a distance. They hold back from immersing themselves in this world.

But others produce writings that make me weep openly in class. A young Hispanic man whose writing so far hasn't been that great (and over the next several weeks continues not to be that great) writes beautifully as the doomed man, and ends, "Let's not waste any more time. I have a train to catch. If it takes me to heaven I'll see my family and friends. And if it takes me to the other place, well, I have friends there, too." A woman also writes as Fortino Samano, as he focuses on his hand in his pocket, rubbing his thumb against his forefinger. He cannot give the order to fire until he names to himself the texture he is remembering: the ear of his dog when he was a child. A student at prison who is a Mexican national uses his own childhood to become a young boy awakened that morning to see the most exciting thing ever to happen in his village. Other Mexican nationals move seamlessly from English narrative to Spanish dialog they have to translate for me. One student is a bullet pulled from a pouch, hoping that when his time comes he isn't a dud. And another student writes as a member of the firing squad, who, after contrasting the courage of the rebel with the supercilious contempt (and fear upon which this is based) of his commanding officer and after firing the fatal bullet, begins to walk, and never stops walking till he reaches the rebel camp.

I show them another photograph, this of Russians looking over some of the 176,000 bodies of civilians massacred by Nazis at the Crimean town of Kerch. These stories, too, are good. Many write as a woman recognizing the face of her son. Some write as the dead son reassuring his mother. One is a ray of gray sunlight reflecting off a mud- and blood-filled puddle.

A student asks, "Do you have something about death?"

"I don't think so. Why do you ask?"

"You're not going to do that annoying child thing to me, are you?"

"Why do you ask that?" I pause. "No, I'm kidding."

"Those two pictures."

I think a moment, then say, "Writing is really about moments of transition. Life to death. Birth. Changes in relationship. Changes in understanding. Great transformations are the stuff of great writing."

"Then why don't you show a picture of someone graduating?"

"First, I don't think that's as big a transition, obviously, and I think it's generally easier to write about more rather than less dramatic transformations. But there's something else, too, which is that I think we in our culture have an odd relationship with death. We simultaneously make it more and less than what it is. We act as though it's not a part of our daily lives. We fear it, deny it, pretend it will never happen to us, live our lives as though it can only happen to someone else, someone we don't know, or as though there's always a tomorrow. We put up with shit we would never put up with, were we connected to the fact we would one day die. And at the same time we don't give death the respect it deserves. Think about what happens in movies. People are killed all the time, seldom with any reckoning of the personal costs. I remember seeing a scene in one of the *Die Hard* movies—I think it was the fifteenth installment—in which Mel Gibson is in an SUV with a woman and child. They're stopped at a train crossing, and the bad guys pull up behind them. There's a horrible shootout that ends, if I recall, with the bad guys somehow getting smashed by the train. Through the whole scene I kept thinking, *This kid will have night-mares for the rest of his life*. He's in for years of counseling. Never mind the woman. Never mind the families of the bad guys. And certainly never mind the Mel Gibson character, who is, as is true of almost all heroes in action movies, at the very least a sociopath, and more likely a psychopath."

"So," the student said, "you want us to think about death differently?"

"I don't care *how* you think about it. It's just that death hangs around every corner, and I think that's something worth thinking about."

The man who cannot think for himself, going beyond what other men have learned or thought, is still enslaved to other men's ideas. Obviously the goal of learning to think is even more difficult than the goal of learning to learn. But difficult as it is we must add it to our list. It is simply not enough to be able to get up a subject of one's own, like a good encyclopedia employee, even though any college would take pride if all its graduates could do so. To be fully human means in part to think one's own thoughts, to reach a point at which, whether one's ideas are different from or similar to other men's, they are one's own.

—Wayne C. Booth

significance

Today I bring a paper sack to class. In it is a photograph, a bullet, some track spikes, and a banana. I place them on a desk in front of me, show each briefly to the class. Then I hand the bullet to the student on my right, who looks at it, then passes it on around the circle. I do the same with the track spikes. I leave the banana on the desk and stand, holding the photograph. I walk around the inside of the circle, showing it to the students. I ask, "What is this?"

They try to stifle laughs.

I say, "You can say it."

"It's a bunch of geeks wearing polyester suits."

"Look at their hair," says another. "It's outrageous. They look like clowns."

I respond, "These were my friends."

Another says immediately, "You were friends with the Partridge Family?"

"No," says another, "His friends were in the circus."

I tell them they can laugh all they want at my expense. "Because I control your grades," I say, "I'm bound to get the last laugh."

"But you don't," one responds.

"Oh, damn. Well, in that case quit laughing."

They don't.

I say, "No. This is not merely some stylin' dudes from the seventies. This is my seventeenth summer, the summer of 1978. This is magic. Swimming, pinball, softball, first kiss—"

A student interrupts to ask which of these guys was the lucky one.

"What's this?" I ask, then point to the bullet, which has gone all the way around the class.

The policeman who does civil disobedience on the side slips unthinkingly into a Jack Webb voice: "It's a live round for a small-caliber handgun. It's relatively old, as you can tell by the slight discoloration, the tarnishing of the brass."

I say, "Correct as far as it goes, but ultimately . . ." I pause. "No."

Eyebrows go down all across the room. Lots of frowns. They don't know what the hell I'm talking about.

"This is a weekend when I was six or seven. One hot afternoon my big brother was lying in bed reading, and I was sitting on the bed next to him. I don't know why he had bullets on the night-stand, and I know even less why I popped one in my mouth. But I did. It went too far back, and I swallowed it."

The eyebrows go back up. Eyes widen. Someone asks, "What did you do?"

"I spent the entire weekend in bed. I was a precocious child, with lots of energy I was always willing to put to mischevious— my siblings would probably say *annoying*—ends. Whenever my brother, who was almost ten years older than I, would bring home a girlfriend to meet the family, I would rush up and ask, as loudly as I could, 'Are you going to kiss her, Rik? Are you going to kiss her now?' It took him a while to come up with a retort, which was, 'Sandy, I'd like you to meet my little brother. Poor thing, he's been this way since birth.' Then there was the time he brought a girlfriend to what he thought was an empty house: my parents and siblings were gone, and I was at a neighbor's house but came back to get something. I heard them making out, so I crawled up behind the couch. Suddenly I leapt up and said, 'Hey Rik! Are you glad to see me?'"

A student asks, "What did you do then?"

"What do you think? I ran for my life."

Another student says, "I would have killed you."

"Well," I say, "That brings us back to the bullet, and why I spent the weekend in bed. Somehow I got the idea that if I moved too fast I'd explode. Now, I'm *not* saying one of my siblings put this idea into my head. I am, however, saying that everyone in the house was glad for the quiet weekend."

They smile, laugh, and then there's silence. I can see their minds working. There's something they don't understand. Finally one of them asks, "How . . . how did you end up with the bullet? How did it come out?"

"Oh, the usual way."

They look at their hands.

I say, "I was so worried I was going to blow up that my mom checked for me everytime I went. Eventually she found it and fished it out for me." I point to the spiikes, pause, then say, "Now, what are *these*?"

They're starting to get it. They know I was in track. One says, "This is your best jump ever."

Another, "It was a hot day and you were really pumped because it was the final meet of the season."

"It's butterflies in your stomach."

Another, a guy who runs track himself, says, "Forget the butter-flies. Have you ever seen female high jumpers? They're the best!"

I tell him I went to a college that was 83 percent male.

He laughs. "So that's why you went out for track. . . ."

"This is great," I say. "These are all of those things. Except the women. I never did date any jumpers, although I agree they're the best looking on the track team. Of course we can say the same about the males, at least in my case."

They laugh. I'm hurt.

"It's something else, too. It's being the best. When I was a child and teenager, I often undercut my own achievements, feeling that I got lucky, or that there was some external reason that I succeeded: The umpire had a generous strike zone when I was pitching, my opponents in basketball had an off day, and so on. I always looked for ulterior motives when people gave me praise. Now, we can talk all we want about how if someone is emotionally healthy external validation isn't necessary—just doing the best you can is supposed to be enough—but I know what I felt I needed, and I know the effect validation had when I got it. That's what track did for me. I was the best. And I couldn't undercut my achievements: The bar stayed up. I simply couldn't argue with that. So, I can tell you a story about a track meet—I can take you there so you feel the heat coming off the track, you smell the high jump pit, hear the starting gun for the sprints, the sound of the officials at the long-jump pit shouting 'mark,' and the clatter of the bar when a high jumper knocks it off—but that's only the first step. I've got to give the story a point, give it some meaning.

"You've done an absolutely wonderful job so far of taking the reader there in your essays and stories—I'm with you every step of the way—and now you're ready for the next step, which is to give readers a reason to care. I'm sure you've all hung out with people who give you every gory detail of their day, or of something that happened ten years ago, and you don't know why they're going on and on and on, and you just want to scream, 'Get to the point!' You want them to give you some emotional content, emotional richness. It's the same when you're telling the story. You want to not only take the readers there—like me just showing you the track spikes—but you also want to let them know what it *means* to you. And you've got to make it mean something to them."

They're quiet. I think they get it. At last someone says, "And what does the banana symbolize?"

"That's my lunch," I say.

~

There's something else I need to say about praise in the classroom. Not only is it important to me that the praise I give always be true, but it's also important that it be unconditional. That's not to say it can't be specific: It must be that. But it would never have helped my students for me to praise only papers I liked. All the research I've read on the subject states unequivocally that conditional praise inhibits creativity. It causes the recipient to move outside him- or herself and toward the teacher, to follow praise instead of the muse.

I found something to praise in every paper. Yes, I was still imposing my ideals of what is good writing by focusing on the parts of their papers I liked best, but I was very clear that more than praising the writing I was praising them as writers, and more than praising them as writers I was praising them as human beings.

Students often wrote papers with politics I didn't much care for. I praised these as much as I did papers with politics more to my liking. One of my students spent a good part of the quarter writing encomia for Ronald Reagan. I helped him improve his logic and speech (it speaks to the air of acceptance in the classroom that he had respectful, lively, and fun political discussions with a woman in class who'd thrown a celebratory party the day Reagan got shot). Similarly, although I don't like alcohol, one student, a wine salesman by trade, wrote nothing but advertisements for wine. I was glad to set my personal issues aside and help him in a way he needed to be helped, and was even more glad he was able to put to larger use the work he did in class.

I never pretended I didn't have preferences, or that I didn't have politics. I stated them upfront. But I made clear to my students that my affection for them wasn't dependent upon their agreement with me. Nor, and this was something we all liked very much about the check-mark system, were their grades affected by whether or not we agreed.

I still remember one paper that gave me more difficulty than any other. It was by a man who had recently attended a bachelor party at his frat house. He described a couple of strippers dancing for a circle of fraternity members. One danced close above the groom, who was sitting in a chair. He bit her on the groin, painfully enough she had to stop and leave the room. When she came back, the two women danced only together, and simulated sex. My student wrote that he was enthralled, and also that it was one of the most perverted things he'd ever seen: "I don't understand why they did it with each other when they could have had any of us. They must be perverts."

When I finished reading I was so angry at this man and the culture that perpetuates these attitudes and practices that I was shaking. I wanted to shake him. There are circumstances in which such a response would have been appropriate. But my awareness of the power differential between teacher and student stopped me. I will never forget the college professor who told me in class that I was a "stupid weasel who doesn't care about anything," nor will I forget how that made me feel. Teachers have power over students; that power brings with it the responsibility to use it appropriately. I was glad I read this paper at home, because it took me a day or so to come up with what I considered to be an appropriate response: "This paper raises many interesting issues. I'm wondering especially about the question of perversion. These women were getting paid to do a job—they were, in essence, acting—and the men in the room were paying to watch them (and evidently at least one person thought he'd also bought the right to bite them). Why does this make the women perverts? I'm wondering also where respect fits into this picture. What is the relationship between respect and sexuality? Where does respect fit into relationships between men and women?"

I'd like to say I changed this man's attitudes toward women, changed his future relationships, changed his life, but I have no idea how he responded to this. He never rewrote the paper, and he and I never discussed it.

I also was very careful about the way I publicly praised students. I know how good it felt as a student (and how good it still feels as a human being) to be praised in public, and at the same time I remember how bad it felt when others were consistently singled out for praise in the classroom and I was not. I remember the excitement I felt when a teacher read something I wrote in front of class, and, once again, the unease I felt as she read through a small stack and got ever closer to the bottom without reading mine. So at the beginning of every quarter I told my students that I would in time publicly read excerpts from everyone's papers, and that they should mark on their papers if they did not want me to read from it aloud (of course I told them also that if the paper contained anything that could conceivably make them feel vulnerable or exposed, that I'd ask them before reading it). I wanted no one to feel left out.

This—trying to create an atmosphere where students feel comfortable enough to begin to explore the contents of their own skin—may all seem a lot of work, but it's not. It's simply showing respect, and affection. And it's certainly less work than moving bees, bucking bales, or busing tables, all of which I've done for cash. As my students continued to blossom (as writers, thinkers, human beings), I kept thinking how easy this work really is, and how if my students had consistently been accepted and loved for who they are by the adults in their lives—by their parents, teachers, school counselors, members of their churches—I would have had to get a real job.

~

I'm fully aware that my gender gives me advantages in teaching the way I do (I'm also fully aware that my gender gives me advantages in almost every aspect of my life). It's relatively easy to surrender authority when I carry in my chromosomes a marker that makes it (culturally) inherent. It helps also that I'm white, and that I'm fairly tall. Each of these attributes is vested by the culture with enough power that I could remove the more external vestments as easily and ultimately with as little threat to my authority as I did my suit jacket.

Were I a woman, this surrender of authority might have been seen as a sign of weakness. That's too bad, because there are people (lots of them) who perceive the world as a never-ending struggle for power (that is, who are very frightened), and who are therefore more likely—whether student, instructor, administrator, or anyone else—to attempt to exploit this perceived weakness, and generally be a pain in the ass. Note, by the way, that I'm not saying that to rebel against authority is necessarily to be a pain in the ass, although there are times it's certainly uncomfortable for all concerned. I'm saying that there are people, once again, lots of them, who are uncomfortable—whether they admit it or not, and frankly the ones who don't admit it are harder to deal with—with women holding any sort of power over them, and who are tempted to show themselves one-up on any woman who does not cling to the external trappings and internal rigidity of power, that is, any woman who does not comport herself like Margaret Thatcher, that is, like a man in a dress. Of course many whites would similarly resent nonwhites holding power over them.

It's not quite true that I surrendered authority, anyway. It would be more accurate to say I set some of it aside. But I certainly kept it within reach, the psychological equivalent of the alarm I wear on my belt at the prison. The check-mark system was a step in the right direction, but I still imposed it from outside. I still took roll. I still determined the classroom agenda, and though I didn't use it, I still had the power to flunk anyone I chose, for any reason I chose.

And let's be honest about my role in class discussions. I can say all I want about trying to run an egalitarian classroom, but the truth is that what I say, on almost any subject, carries far more weight in my classroom than what any other individual might say. A teacher speaks, and students pay more attention than if another student says the same thing, or something that refutes it. I remember, to take a trivial example, my seventh-grade science teacher telling us all that it's possible to drink enough water to fill up your stomach and esophagus, and then to walk over to a sink, lean your face forward, and pour the water back out. If one of my friends had said that, I would have disbelieved and disremembered it pretty quickly. But because my teacher said it, I believed it at the time, and still remember. The same can be said for many other equally absurd things my teachers said, including most of what was taught in math, science, history, economics, and so on.

And aren't I pushing an agenda, too, simply by my choice of what we talk about in class? Am I not making a political statement by choosing to have them write about the execution of a revolutionary? Would I not be making a different statement by showing pictures of Wall Street traders, Marines planting a flag on Iwo Jima (or shooting civilians in the Philippines, Korea, Vietnam, Panama, Grenada, Somalia, Iraq, Afghanistan, and so on, essentially ad infinitum)? Of course any picture I present—any action I take or do not take—is intensely political, even if only for what it ignores. What if I present the façade of running an apolitical class and show a picture of a smiling (white, heterosexual, upper-middle class, nuclear) family sitting down for a

Thanksgiving turkey dinner? That would, of course, present my students with one side of a picture, and point them toward writing their way down one particular path. Showing them a picture of that turkey living out its short, wretched life in a factory farm and asking them to write about that would take them down a different path, as would showing them a line drawing of Indians slaughtered by these same Pilgrims whose giving of thanks we commemorate.

Of course the teacher is going to have more voice in a classroom. That's one reason it's so crucial for me not to grade papers: I need to delink my opinions (political and otherwise) from the very real coercive power of grades.

This question of grades being coercive, and of politics being inherent in teaching, applies not only to writing, but to all fields. Mathematics, science, economics, history, religion, are all just as deeply and necessarily political. To believe they're not—to believe, for example, that science (or mathematics, economics, history, religion, and so forth: choose your poison) describes the world as it is, rather than acting as a filter that removes all information that does not fit the model and colors the information that remains—is in itself to take a position, one that is all the more powerful and dangerous because it is invisible to the one who holds it.

～

*Security is mostly a superstition. It does not
exist in nature, nor do the children of men as
a whole experience it. Avoiding danger is no
safer in the long run than outright exposure.
Life is either a daring adventure, or nothing.*
—Helen Keller

～

giving up control

I think that when I'm eighty-three, looking back over a life spent successfully working to dismantle the psychological and physical infrastructures of civilization, unbinding humans and nonhumans alike from this enslavement, I'll still be telling young children—who, incomprehensibly enough to those of us born a couple of generations earlier, will be living in a world with *more* wild salmon returning each year, *more* migratory songbirds, *more* monarch butterflies, where herds of bison steadily grow, as do towns of prairie dogs, as do great complex communities of grasslands, marshes, and forests, where roads crumble, skyscrapers tumble, and cars rust away—about the Great Chalkboard War of 1995. Perhaps we'll sit talking on an old floating dock at the mouth of Elk Creek as the tide, which had ebbed as low as I've ever seen it, slowly rises. They've heard the story before, so they already know the unfamiliar terms: chalkboard, custodian, vacuuming, school.

I'll begin, "I remember it just like it was yesterday. I was teaching a night class at the time, and one evening when I walked in I saw that someone had written in bold letters on a chalkboard at the side of the room: 'Put the chairs back in rows!'"

"What a silly thing," one of the children will say.

I'll nod, then continue, "The exclamation point kind of bothered me, as did the lack of a *please*. I left his words on the board, and wrote in somewhat smaller letters below: 'Who is making this request? If you're a custodian, I'll gladly do it. If not, I'll make a deal: you put them in a circle for us, and we'll put them in rows for you.'"

Another child will say, "That sounds like a fair deal to me."

I'll continue, "A couple of years before, a custodian wrote a note on the board saying that leaving the chairs in a circle made vacuuming harder. Of course, after that we returned the chairs to rows. But then came budget cuts, and the janitorial staff was laid off, the work subcontracted. I noticed a few months later that the vacuuming ceased entirely: dropped candy wrappers, pencil stubs, pieces of paper, flakes of mud, all remained throughout the quarter. That was the end of returning chairs to rows.

"The next evening another message had been added to the board, still in strong letters: 'Don't be immature. Grow up and put the chairs the way they belong.'

"I wrote, 'Students—and by extension chairs—don't belong in rows. And I wouldn't call the questioning of authority or tradition immature, but rather a sign of emotional and psychological well-being. If we learn nothing else from the horrors of the Holocaust, Vietnam, and the ongoing destruction of the planet, we should learn that blind obedience to authority or tradition is far more problematical than any questioning a person might do, don't you think?'

"Many of my students arrived early the next night, eager to read the coming installment. The mysterious professor did not disappoint: 'Cut this nonsense out. This is a school, and I'm trying to teach something here.'

"I wrote back: 'I am, too. That's why I'm doing this. The question becomes: What are you teaching?'

"I pictured students all through the day coming to their classes, watching this ongoing debate. I hoped I was setting little fires of rebellion in people I'd never meet. Or maybe they thought I was making something of nothing. I'll never know. I know many of my students loved it, and learned a lot from it."

One of the children will ask, "Why do you think they learned a lot from it?"

I'll say, "They told me."

The child will ask, "If you were never going to meet these other students, why did you care if you lighted fires of rebellion in them?"

"Two reasons. The first was that the culture was killing the planet and harming the vast majority of humans as well—and I can't tell you how good it feels to use the past tense in that statement—and so needed to be brought down. The second was more personal. So many people weren't happy, weren't following their hearts, in part because we had entire institutions such as schools and universities (and really the whole culture) set up in great measure specifically to lead people away from themselves—to seduce them—and so it never occurred to most of them to seriously question the paths laid out for them by someone else (their parents, schools, the economic system). I know that when I was in school, I was miserable, and I looked for any lifeline, any sign I wasn't crazy for wanting to follow my own heart and that the culture was crazy for rewarding me not to. Seeing an exchange like the one on the chalkboard would have helped me immeasurably when I was in college. If I could help these students ask questions about something so simple as having desks in rows, and show them someone standing up to this sort of meaningless, unthinking authority, perhaps some of them would follow those questions wherever they led. And that's a beautiful thing, because once the questions start they never stop."

A child will ask, "Why would parents and teachers or anyone else try to get children to do things that don't make them happy?"

"Ah," I'll say, "You're playing the Annoying Child game, aren't you?"

And the children will laugh.

I'll continue, "The next night there was another message: 'I'm not going to waste any more time debating with a fool. If the chairs are not back in rows tomorrow morning, I'm going to your supervisor.'

"One of my students said, 'Those are fighting words, Derrick. Are you going to call him out?' A few wanted me to not respond at all, because they didn't want me to get in trouble. I told them that earlier, talking to my supervisor about something else (fishing, to be precise), I'd mentioned the chalkboard war. My supervisor asked if I wanted him to check the room schedules to make sure I wasn't rattling the wrong cage, and I told him it didn't matter which cage it was, I wanted to rattle it. He'd said, 'Rattle away.'

"But I wasn't sure what to do. It seemed the chalkboard discussion was moving from a struggle over ideas into a pissing contest. That didn't interest me at all. I thought I'd made my point. It was also crucial, however, that I not stop the discourse right then, because I didn't want students—especially those who might be following the additions outside of my class—to think his threat of going to a higher power had carried the day: that would be precisely the wrong note on which to end the lesson. I thought for a couple of minutes, then realized there was another point I wanted to make to my own students anyway, this having to do with strategies of discourse. I wrote, 'If I may for a moment shift from a discussion of issues to one of tactics, I'd like to point out that while attacking the person one disagrees with—either through name-calling (e.g., "immature," "fool") or through some sort of threat (e.g., "I'm going to your supervisor")—instead of confronting the substance of the other's arguments is certainly a tactic with a long and storied tradition, it is often a tool of last resort, because it shows the weakness of the user's arguments. If the user were able to construct a case, he wouldn't need to call names or make threats: He could merely make his case. Furthermore, name-calling violates a fundamental principle of good writing, which is "Show, don't tell." Calling someone a fool is not good writing. It's much better to have someone read what you've written—whether it's in an article or book or on a chalkboard—and then have the reader say, "That guy he's describing really is a fool." *That* is good writing.'

"The next day all of the writing on the chalkboard had been erased. For the rest of the quarter we went ahead and put the chairs in rows."

The children laugh and laugh. The tide continues to come in, continues to raise the dock on which we sit.

~

I'm not suggesting anyone else try to run a class the way I do. To suggest that would manifest a disrespect normally reserved for students, who by this point more or less expect under our system to be formed and deformed into shapes that bear very little resemblance to the people beneath, the people they really are. That's the industrial model, where we try to force everyone into the same mold. That may be good for industrial production, but it's hell on the psyche (as well as the planet). And it just doesn't work. For example, I can't write press releases. For years in Spokane I did a lot of writing and editing for an environmental organization. If they wanted flowing prose, I was their go-to guy. But when they asked me to write press releases I'd sit there for hours, agonizing over language that they would never be able to use anyway. And my experience with press releases was good compared to what happened the night they asked me to help with a phone tree. It's not me. I couldn't do it. I sat there for a couple of hours, dialing the first six digits of someone's phone number, then freezing and finding myself unable to finish the call. If the FBI or CIA ever decides to arrest me for my work against the system, they needn't bother attaching electrodes to my genitals: they can just force me to cold-call strangers.

The task we all face as human beings (and I'm sure trees face similar tasks, as do frogs, rocks, stars, fires, gusts of wind, kisses, caresses, and pieces of art) is to find and become who we are. The task teachers face is to find their own way of teaching, one that manifests who they are. This, of course, means they first have to gain some understanding of who resides in their skin.

About halfway through my first quarter at Eastern, my supervisor told me, "Early on I was worried about you, and how you'd be in the classroom. I liked what you said, but I didn't know if you were for real. And I knew that if you didn't walk your talk, students would spot it in a hot minute, and both you and they would be in for a hard time. We can't fool them. We may think we can, but they're smarter than we usually give them credit for."

So here is what I'm suggesting: that teachers think about what they're doing, and about the personal and political implications of their subject matter; that they try to understand who they themselves are; and that they attempt to follow their own daimons in their own classrooms. Here is what else I'm suggesting: that no matter the subject matter ostensibly being taught, the real point is to help the students find themselves, and to find their own passion. Anything else is to lead them astray, to do them actual damage.

~

I still had too much control of the class. My best writing comes when I give up control, let the piece lead me where it will. No, *lead* is too solid a word, as though the muse is walking sedately a step ahead of me, holding my hand and gently pulling. Instead, the act of writing, when I allow it to be its best, reminds me of nothing so much as something I loved as a child and teenager, which was to run down rocky mountains as fast as I could. I'd start at the top, then begin trotting, picking up speed with gravity until my body was very nearly moving faster than my legs could churn, and certainly faster than I was able to pick out safe spaces for my feet to land. I'd hurdle downed logs and large rocks, trusting in my eyes and in my feet and in the ground itself that I'd be able to negotiate whatever was on the far side. Of course I tripped often, but that taught me how to fall without hurting myself too much, to roll and regain my feet and start over in one swift motion. Going back further, I can remember as a small child—five, six, seven years old—running down great sand dunes hundreds of feet high in southern Colorado. I'd fly off the top of a ridge and run faster and faster until my feet could no longer keep up, and then I'd tumble and tumble all the way down (frankly just thinking about that part makes me nauseated at this point: my stomach must have been much stronger as a child). I've been told that when I cleared the top of a ridge, the biggest things on me were my eyes, opening wider and wider from simultaneous fear and delight. That (apart from the nausea) is what I want in my writing, that's what I want in my life, and that's what I want in my classroom.

How would I do that?

Finally it occurred to me to break the students into groups, and ask each group to run the class for one two-hour period (students in day classes had only one hour to work with). They could do almost anything they wanted. I insert the word *almost* because every quarter I had to dissuade at least one group from having the entire class play nude Twister. But almost anything else was fair game. One group wanted to play capture the flag. I thought, "What does *this* have to do with writing?" But we did it, then wrote about it, and I felt closer to that class after our group's physical activity than I had even after intense emotional discussions. During the next class period we talked about the relationship between shared physical activities and feelings of intimacy. Another group had us eat popsicles and watch cartoons, then draw pictures from our childhood with our opposite hands (it broke my heart when one fellow shared his picture with the class: "This is my father taking me out in the woods to smoke my first vial of crack"). In the same group we played duck duck goose and hide-and-go-seek in the basement of the near-empty building. Many of the people were continuing students, and thus were older. Looking back, I don't know how anyone could possibly say that he or she has successfully run a writing class without having played hide-and-go-seek with overweight old men, twenty-year-olds, middle-aged mothers of five, and a half-dozen men and women whose native language is not English, all of them dead serious about finding or not being found.

Another group brought a bag of questions and handed one to each of us. Each person would answer the proffered question, and then we'd go around the room all giving our answers. Then to the next person's question, and so on. The questions were excellent. Mine was, "How do you want to die?"

One group included a Vietnam vet. On their night he and one other student wrote on one chalkboard the words *patriotism*, *heroism*, *war*, *bomb*, *national defense*, *national interest*, *missiles*, *tanks*, *guns*, *helicopters*, *soldiers*, *generals*. Simultaneously two other group members wrote on another chalkboard, right next to the first, the words *fuck*, *prick*, *cunt*, *sex*, *come*, *tit*. We went around the room giving our reactions to the words on the two lists. The point soon became clear: Why, they were asking, are the words on the second list considered obscene while the first are not?

In a class run by another group, we went around the circle saying the thing we did in our lives we were the most ashamed of. It would have been easy for people to share only superficial acts had the group members not gone first. One had as a child playfully tied a string around a kitten's neck, forgotten about it, and come back a half hour later to find that the string had caught on the edge of the sofa when the kitten jumped off, and the kitten was dead. A man told us of infidelity to his wife. After that, there was no holding back. We were most of us in tears before we got around the circle.

One group taught us how to do a country-and-western dance, the Tush Push. This was especially difficult for me, a confirmed nondancer. Because the room was too small, we did this in the building's central courtyard. Midway through one of our times pushing our respective tushes, a couple of the department's most humorless administrators walked by, evidently having worked into the evening. I smiled and waved. Even this class taught me much. I had been working on letting go in my writing for years by this point, and I sometimes became frustrated at the baby steps many students were taking toward manifesting their passion in words. But when it came to me attempting to let go in dancing, I suddenly comprehended their inhibitions: I would push my tush only three or four inches, while many who were too shy to open up in words were wildly swinging their hips (including a fifty-year-old sheriff's deputy I never would have pegged for a tush-pusher).

In another class we made marshmallow figures representing our hopes and dreams. One fellow, a bow hunter, made a big marshmallow buck with toothpick antlers, and a huge toothpick arrow jutting from its chest; mine was a broken marshmallow dam with marshmallow salmon swimming in a river of marsh-mallow. We played blindfolded soccer in the classroom, with four people at a time blindfolded, being told where to move by sighted partners ("Left, left," my partner shouted as I ran into the wall. "Oh, sorry, wrong way."). We broke into groups, each group picking out of a hat the rough plot for a screenplay (our group was to come down from a mountain to find that everyone else in the world had disappeared), and then each person in the group picked from a different hat a character to be played in the drama (I was to play the actress Sharon Stone), after which we had an hour to write our scripts and to perform what we later dubbed "An Exercise in Embarrassment." For Halloween, we plopped sleeping bags on the floor, sat around a flashlight surrounded by small pieces of wood (simulating a campfire), ate s'mores, and told ghost stories. For Valentine's Day, we wrote stories about first loves, and memories of hearts broken or overflowing. Mainly we had fun.

～

I was required by the department to give an in-class midterm exam. The regulations, however, included nothing about *grading* the exam, which gave me the opening I wanted to try something fun. A couple of days before the midterm I asked the students to write down questions they'd like to see answered. The next period I emptied a trashcan and walked round the circle holding it. They put in their questions. I shook up the papers and circulated again. This time they took questions back out. Those who liked their questions now knew what they'd write on for the midterm. Those who didn't like their question put them back for a dispersal draft. Those who still didn't tried again. And again. Those who never did get one they liked made up their own.

The next class they came in ready to write. I told them I'd be watching them carefully to make sure they didn't copy off each other. The class period after that I read a little from each paper.

The quality of questions ran from deeply thoughtful and thought-provoking to those of the "Oh, shit, class starts in five minutes" variety. Many questions were personal: What is your first memory? Were you happy as a child? When is the happiest you've ever been? Have you known someone who died? Have you seen a birth? When were you the most scared? Some were political: Is the U. S. political system salvageable? Should Bush and the United States invade Iraq? (It's interesting that someone asked that question in a class in 1991, and I'm sure if I were still teaching at Eastern in 2003 someone would have asked the same question.) Many were spiritual or religious: Do you believe in God? What is God? Is there a relationship between your belief/disbelief in God and your personal sense of morality?

I was more or less constantly struck by the hunger so many—though of course not all—students have for depth, substance, meaning. They often asked real questions, and often gave real answers. I remember one student was asked the not very interesting question, "Which came first, the chicken or the egg?" I thought he'd toss it and make up one of his own, but he wrote one of the most thoughtful replies I ever saw. He began by saying that because chickens descended from dinosaurs obviously eggs came first. That, I thought, would have been clever enough, but it was only his jump-off point into an extraordinary exploration of the nature of existence, preordination, free will, and fate: Was the chicken already present in the dinosaur? Similarly, were the actions this student now takes as an adult already present in him as a child? What is the relationship between who he is now and who he will be tomorrow? And who is it who continues from day to day? The question came down to: Who am I?

This is all far more interesting, important, and meaningful, I think, than a standardized essay (standardized essays are so much easier to grade!) in which everyone writes for two hours on a topic like secondhand smoke or the joys of shopping at thrift stores.

*"What are ten or fifteen years?" asked the
Mother Superior serenely. "Think of eternity."
I made no answer. I knew that eternity is
each minute that passes.*

—Nikos Kazantzakis

who are you, again?

walk into class. I ask, "How many of you are here tonight?"
Most of them raise their hands. That's a good sign.

"Who is here?"

Those with hands raised keep them up, and a few eyebrows
follow. A couple of the other students now raise their hands, too.

"Who is it who's here?"

Eyebrows fall into frowns.

"Who are you? Who are *you*?"

No one says anything.

"Who are you? I really want to know." Still no one says anything, so I break in to the Who song. It doesn't help them understand. I try again, "When you read a book or take a walk or have
sex or come to class, who is it who is actually doing this thing?"

A student says, shyly, "I am."

Other students laugh in agreement.

"Who is that?"

Another says, "Oh, no! He's doing that thing where no matter
what you say he keeps asking you questions! Run for your life!"

"That's the point," I say. "Who would be running?"

"I would!"

More laughter.

"But who are you?"

No response.

I say, "Ooh, ooh. Ooh, ooh." They don't appreciate my Roger
Daltry impression. "We've talked a lot in this class about being
who you are, but who, or what, is that? A few years ago I read a

book called *Flatland* by Edwin A. Abbott, in which he describes a world with only two dimensions, like a piece of paper. Flatland women, who are as in our culture considered lesser, are straight lines. Men have more sides (and thus more corners), depending on their social rank. The more corners, the higher social esteem you have: pentagons are more highly regarded than squares who are more highly regarded than triangles. It's pretty interesting. They have houses, they have relationships, they have their own perspective, all of which is two-dimensional. Everything beyond that they cannot comprehend. If you were to put a coin on this world, they wouldn't see its height, but could only go around the edge. They couldn't tell if it was a tenth of an inch high or a hundred miles high. In fact the concept of high would never occur to them. It couldn't. Then he describes Lineland, where the entire world consists of a line. And Spaceland, which is more like our world. And worlds with more dimensions than that. But I want to talk about a specific type of creature who might live in Flatland. When it's born it's a small black point. Over time it grows to a larger circle, and then grows a harder, tan-colored skin when it's a teenager. Later, as it reaches adulthood it takes on a different color, and its shape becomes hexagonal, corresponding to the status an adult has. That's how it lives most of its life. Toward the end it becomes circular again, and very hard and shiny. When it's extremely near death it loses that color, becomes pale red, and very soft. And then, nothingness."

They stare at me. Perhaps they think I'm repeating the exercise where they're supposed to pretend I'm from Mars.

I say, "Of course I'm describing a pencil moving through a piece of paper. Someone living in the paper, who only comprehends two dimensions (as well as, of course, time), would perceive the point as a baby, the eraser as someone in senescence. But the truth is that all of the pencil was all there all the time."

Someone asks, "What's the point?"

"A baby. The other end is the old one."

"No, what's the point of you telling us this?"

"What if we're the same way, one big, long being—*big* and *long* being three-dimensional words for a four- or five-dimensional being—who is a baby on one end and an old person on the other, passing through this three-dimensional space we think of as everything there is?"

"You really believe that?"

"Of course not. Everyone knows our bodies aren't really where we live: our bodies are kind of like TV or radio receivers. Imagine if you'd never seen a television before, and you walked into a room and saw it on. You might think the Red Sox and the Mariners are actually a bunch of little people running around inside, as though it's a tiny stage or a tiny world. You remember those old RCA Victor ads where the dog thinks a human being is talking, but it's really a record player, right?"

Most don't remember. Some don't remember record players.

I continue nonetheless, "Maybe we only think our bodies are where the action takes place, but instead our bodies are complex receivers that play out the energy that's everywhere, kind of like the radio and television waves that surround us but do not become perceptible to us until the waves encounter receivers tuned to the right frequency."

"You mean space aliens beam us into existence?"

"No, silly, life itself. It's dancing and exploding all around us, and when the right wavelength meets the right vessel, boom, there you go, instant animation. Instant person. Or tree or frog or rock. All each of us is doing is manifesting in our own particular way the life force that surrounds us all. We don't really think with our brains, anymore than the Mariners live inside a television. That's just where it comes into focus."

"So that's what you really believe."

"Of course not. The truth is that who I am is an invisible, weightless thing called a soul that lives way out somewhere beyond the stars, in a place called heaven. I took on physical form only as a test to determine whether I would follow the rules laid down by the King—and I don't mean Elvis—and if I do then I get to go back and live in heaven forever, strumming on harps and eating manna—which, by the way, some biblical scholars think was insect exudate—while conversing with other people who passed the test. And it's very definitely pass/fail. No check marks here. If I fail, I burn forever. I'm not sure whether it will be my physical form or my soul that will burn. If it's the soul, I guess the fires, too, are invisible. That was a huge point of contention in the Catholic Church a thousand years ago: whether the fires of hell were spiritual or physical. The two sides in that debate eventually agreed to disagree, each side sure the other would find out soon enough."

"You've said you're not a Christian, so I know you don't believe that one."

"He said he's not a Christian?" someone else asks. We pause a moment, wait for the building to collapse, or at least for the electricity to go out.

"No, I don't believe that one either. Instead we all know that who I am is an ego in a sack of skin. I stop at my fingertips. Everything inside of this sack is me. Or at least most of it is: If I get the flu, those viruses aren't me. And I'm not sure whether the bacteria in my gut are me or if they're not. Maybe if they're helpful to me, they're part of me, and if not, then they're not me. And what about the food I ate an hour ago? Is that me or not? By the time it's my blood it's me. I think. But if I bleed it's not me anymore. A few years ago I had part of my intestine removed. I kept wondering afterward which part was me: the intestine or the rest of me. If the rest of me is me, at what point did the intestine become not part of me? Maybe when they cut it out. Because everything else in the world outside of me isn't me. None of you are me."

"But," one of the students says, "what about your memories of us? Are they you?"

"Yes, I suppose they are," I say. "Except that I can think of some people in my past whose memories are more like the viruses I mentioned."

Another: "And what about the air I just breathed out, and now you're breathing in? Who is that?"

"Sometimes," a woman says, "my sister and I think the same things at the same time, even when we're miles apart. How does that fit in?"

"That's just coincidence," a man says.

"It happens all the time," she responds.

Another: "That's because you were raised together, and having had the same inputs you're going to provide the same outputs at the same times."

"Like a machine," I say.

"Well, yes."

"I forgot to tell you," I say, "That I really think we're nothing more than machines built to propagate our genes. Everything else is secondary."

"You don't believe that."

"You're right. We're actually a web of relationships and experiences. I'm the intersection of every person in class right now, along with everything I've ever experienced, every breath I've ever taken, every word I've ever spoken, every piece of food I've ever eaten. I'm not a *thing* at all. I'm a process. I'm not even that. I can't be described in our language because sentences require a noun and a verb. Most of them. Lightning strikes. But what is lightning? It's not a thing that strikes. It's a process. So am I."

"What happens," another woman asks, "if you have sex and you take someone into your body? Are they then part of you?"

"I have memories," says another (this a woman who has written much about having been raped), "that affect me every day. I don't want those memories to be part of me, but they are. I wish I could get rid of them—make them not part of me—but I can't."

"If my son died," the man who wrote about the chicken and the egg says, "I would die, too. He's a part of me."

A woman says, "I heard laughter the moment my grandmother died. And she loved to laugh. She was a thousand miles away, and I heard it. I knew it was her, and I knew she had just died."

The students are off and running. I really don't need to say much else for the rest of the class period.

~

It's the next class period. That same student asks yet again, "What was the point of that last exercise?"

The class laughs.

My eyes open wide. I ask him, "Who are you?"

*Unless I know what sort of doorknob his
fingers closed on, how shall I—satisfactorily
to myself—get my character out of doors?*
—Ford Madox Ford

clarity

The seventh rule of writing is that you want the reader to think about what you want the reader to think about, and you don't want the reader to think about what you don't want the reader to think about. Read that again.

On the simplest level, this means you want to be clear. You don't, for example, want to write, "Jim and Bob were talking, and he said . . ." You want readers to think about what Jim or Bob would say; you don't want them wondering which character is talking. Unless of course you do. On this level it means being precise.

Now let's move to another level. When I was younger, my mom worked in the American Indian section of the Denver Art Museum, and also worked for a time as an agent for Indian artists. So I learned a lot about native cultures. The upshot of this was that when I watched westerns as a child I wasn't thinking about whether the cavalry would save the pioneers from being scalped by Indians—which is presumably what the directors wanted me to think about—because instead my mother was saying, "Plains Indians didn't wear Hopi decorations. And look, that one's dressed like an Iroquois! And did you see that bear claw necklace on the other one? That's crazy! That's an Iowa grizzly-bear-claw necklace. The ones in eastern Montana were different. Ridiculous." This in a movie where the hero routinely fired ten bullets from a six-shooter, and a pioneer woman just as routinely killed a half-dozen Indians with one shot from an old muzzleloader. And this in a movie where Indians scalp whites, as opposed to the much more historically accurate other way around. So the point of this is that if you're going to spend millions of dollars to make a western, do some research. The same holds true if you're going to write a paper. Do the basic research. Not so you'll get a better grade. So readers will think about what you want them to think about.

These days if I watch a western I'm still not thinking what the director wants me to think: I'm thinking about genocide, and what movies would look like that showed Nazis killing Jews and others if they were written, produced, directed, and acted by Nazis. It's not just westerns. When I see a cop movie I'm thinking these days about pro-police-state propaganda. For example, I just heard there's a new movie coming out about intrepid antiterrorist experts trying to stop anarchists from poisoning the world's water supplies. Were I to watch it, I wouldn't be thinking about the tricks and turns of the case at hand, but instead I'd be reflecting on the fact that no anarchists have ever poisoned any water supplies: It goes against everything all the anarchists I know or have read stand for. The movie would be much more accurate and exciting for me if they slightly change the description: intrepid anarchists try to stop capitalists from poisoning the world's water supplies. Now there's a movie that would have me biting my nails.

The director George Roy Hill was aware of this rule when he created *Butch Cassidy and the Sundance Kid*. He knew that in the final scene he wanted Butch and Sundance to shoot more than six shots from their guns without reloading. He wanted to cheat. But he didn't want viewers to think about that. How did he get around it? Throughout the movie he repeatedly showed the two reloading their weapons. He wanted us to be thinking about the fact that he didn't cheat, precisely so he could when we were no longer looking. It's pretty slick.

Perhaps another way to say this is that you want to anticipate places that may jar readers into remembering that they're reading and not experiencing directly. I wrote a novel a couple of years ago that didn't work. I'll rework it someday. There is a murder in the book. The murder takes place inside, and I didn't want the killers to have to clean up too big a mess. I called a friend's husband who's an emergency-room doctor. (Another writer friend of mine insists that every writer should become friends with a forensic pathologist: I concur, but haven't yet found one.) I asked, "If you were going to shoot someone at close range, and didn't want the bullet to come out the back, what type of gun would you use?" He told me. I asked, "If the guy is shot in the heart, how long does it take him to die? What happens in the meantime?" He told me that, too. He knows me well enough that he was thinking what I wanted him to think (staying focused on technical issues) and not thinking what I didn't want him to think—that I'm one sick pup for asking these questions. Also, it's crucial to the plot that a friend of one of the killers wanders into the room just before the killing. The friend knows nothing of the planned murder. I asked my students at the prison to think about people they know who've killed someone. What would they have done in this situation? Would they abort the killing? Go ahead with it? Kill the witness as well? They said that most would kill the witness. "But that's the difference," one said, "between a cold killer and someone who has something he has to do. There are plenty of people sitting in prison because they weren't cold enough to kill the witnesses, which logically they probably should have done." If it's crucial to the plot that they proceed with the killing, and also that they not kill the friend, I asked, how can I make that convincing? I want readers to be caught up in the plot, not saying, "That would never work that way." My students gave me ideas on how to pull it off.

All of this applies not only to physical facts and activities, but to arguments as well. You want the reader to be with you as you make your case. You don't want your reader either confused or raising objections you don't anticipate and answer.

Someone once asked the Confederate general Nathan Bedford Forrest how he won so many battles. He answered, "You get there first with the most." The same applies in writing. I tell my students that as writers they have to get to their readers' objections before the readers do, and they have to do this so smoothly that the objections never even come up.

~

The eighth rule of writing is what I call the Ranch Dressing lesson. Here's how it goes: Two friends go to dinner. Standing on a sidewalk in front of the restaurant, one says to the other, "What would you like to eat?"

The other responds, "I don't care, so long as I don't have to eat ranch dressing. I hate ranch dressing."

"I never knew you hated ranch dressing."

"I do."

They walk inside, sit down. The waiter asks what they'd like to eat.

The second person says, "It doesn't matter to me, so long as I don't have to eat ranch dressing. I hate ranch dressing."

The waiter says, "I don't think that will be a problem. We have plenty of other foods here."

But when their salads are brought to them, ranch dressing covers the greens.

The man says, "I can't eat this. I hate ranch dressing."

"My apologies," says the waiter. "I'll bring you another, this time with no ranch dressing, since you hate it."

After the meal, the first man asks the second how he enjoyed it.

The second says, "Very much. It was an excellent meal, because I didn't have to eat any ranch dressing. As you may or may not know, I hate ranch dressing."

That's the end of the story. Now here's the lesson: After reading this story, the first thing many readers would say is, "I don't understand. What are you trying to tell me, that the guy doesn't like potatoes? I don't get it."

No matter how clear you may think you're being, the chances are good you're not. And no matter how obvious you think you've made every twist and turn of your argument for the reader, the chances are good you haven't. This isn't because readers are particularly stupid. This difficulty in communicating is inherent in art, and in communication. So far as the former, I cannot tell you how many climaxes to how many movies have failed to convey their full power to me because I've been trying to remember which character is the one I saw three scenes ago, and which is the one I thought died in the first ten minutes of the film; suddenly in those situations I understand—apart from the racism in the choice of colors—why those cheesy westerns had the bad guys wear black hats.

At the prison recently, after a student read his story, I said, "I like the way those two characters interact, but I was finding myself wondering the whole time what's the nature of their relationship. They seem good friends with a large difference in age. How did they meet?"

My student responded, "On page two, I say, 'He looked at his father. . . .'"

"I'm sorry. I didn't hear that."

"On page seven, one calls the other, 'Son.'"

"I thought that was a figure of speech between older and younger men."

We all looked at each other, then said, as if on cue, "Ranch dressing."

There's a larger point to be made here than my own obtuseness, which is the fragility, beauty, and at the same time resilience of any communication. An inchoate impulse forms into a feeling that resembles but can never match the dreamy intensity of the original impulse. This feeling then articulates itself, but the words at best approximate a shadow of the feeling. I speak or write these words, and of course the person who receives them brings to that receiving his or her own connotations: Cinnamon, for example, may conjure different memories and may mean something different for you than for me; the same can be said for sex, civilization, and salmon. These words may then settle into feelings, leading finally, perhaps, to some impulse on your part. With so many layers of interpretation, it's no wonder we so often misunderstand each other. And this is between two people who speak the same language. How much more difficult understanding can be, then, when the people do not share a common cultural background, or native tongue? How much more than this may we misunderstand when we then hear a dog speak, or a tree or stone?

In my twenties, when I was just learning to write, this inability to match in my writing either the beauty or power of the natural world or the intensity of my own dreams—an inability that lasts to this day: no description I can ever write of the late afternoon sunlight striking the yellow, brown, gray and green of long, slender redwood branches and their feathery needles could match the experience of seeing them right now—intimidated me so much it stopped me from writing for a couple of years. But finally one day I realized I was being silly. This realization came as I pulled down an offramp from an interstate. I saw a stop sign, and it occurred to me that just as no one expects a stop sign to stop a car, I shouldn't expect words to substitute for experience. That's not their job, although words certainly can be misused that way. The job of words is to direct us toward experience, to round out experience, to facilitate experience, and to give us ways to share at least pale shadows of that experience with those we love. And the job of words is to help us learn to be—and act—human.

~

I've never kissed my oldest friend. We've often talked about why we never became romantically involved back in our late twenties, and have decided in retrospect—our lives having long since moved in directions that make it inappropriate for us to now get together—that one reason had to do with an inability to read each other's signals. We'd often have intense and delightful conversations, during which I was always struck by how she kept her eyes glued on mine. I knew, mainly from watching movies (as opposed to direct experience: my friends and I were nothing if not nerds) that a primary way a person signals a willingness, nay, eagerness, to kiss is by flickering one's glance from the other's eyes down to lips, and back up. This never happened. I found out later she spoke a different language, where one signals this interest by intently looking at the other's eyes. She had evidently watched different movies than I. So I was sending her a message time and again by looking at her lips, she was sending me the same message just as often by looking at my eyes, and meanwhile we each slept alone. This is an example of the Ranch Dressing lesson in practice.

~

There's another rule of writing, one my students and I have taken to calling *tracking*. We call it that because it involves trying to make sure that as the reader's focus moves from word to word, image to image, argument to argument, it tracks smoothly (except when you want it to not). For example, I can read with pleasure a description by Raymond Chandler of a woman's face. When I go back and read it again, I observe that his description moves not randomly but directionally, from hair to cheeks to lip to chin to neck to breasts. It tracks smoothly. Moving from hair to breasts and back up to face would jerk the reader's focus around, which you only want to do if that's what you want to do, say, if you want to convey that the person looking is nervous or self-conscious about looking.

Probably the easiest examples of tracking come from movies. Let's say you and I are talking, and the camera shows first your face when you speak, and then mine as I do, then yours, and so on. The focus of the audience will go back and forth between us. After one of the times I speak, the camera shows someone sneaking through a door, holding a knife. If this is all the information viewers have been given, they'll have no idea what to feel: The man with the knife could be half a world away. If, on the other hand, the last time I spoke, my gaze jumped briefly from your face to somewhere behind your left shoulder, the viewers' focus will track along with my eyes, and viewers will be more likely to understand that the man with the knife is sneaking up behind you.

I learned about tracking from two people: Alfred Hitchcock and John Keeble. Alfred Hitchcock taught it to me with one scene from *Psycho*. Early on, the film's first protagonist, Marion, steals $40,000 from her employer. We want her to get away with it. As she's leaving town, she sees her boss crossing the street, and we hope he doesn't stop. Later, she sleeps by the road, and a policeman peers into her window. We hope he doesn't see the money in her purse. She gets to a hotel, and is killed in the shower. The next shot is what taught me about tracking: The camera pulls out from a close-up of her unblinking eye, pans across the room to where the money is folded inside a newspaper, back across the room to the open window, then up toward the house that Norman Bates shares with his mother. The next thing we hear is Norman shouting, "Oh God, Mother, blood! Blood!" He then rushes down to the hotel and begins to clean up the aftermath of the killing. He puts Marion's body in the trunk of her car, and as he's putting the cleaning materials in there, too, another car drives by. We in the audience are a little nervous for Norman. He then takes her car out to the swamp behind the motel and pushes it in. The car sinks till only the roof is showing, then stops. I've seen *Psycho* several times in theaters, and each time the audience gasps at this, then laughs in relief as the car finally goes under.

But what just happened? Ten minutes before, we as audience members identified with Marion, and now, suddenly, our identification has switched so thoroughly that we want Norman to get away with cleaning up after her murder. That's an extraordinary piece of artistic manipulation. How did Hitchcock do that? By paying attention to tracking: The shot where he pulls away from her eye literally pulled us out of Marion's consciousness. We then, with the camera, seek another place to project our identification, and the first person we hear is Norman.

John Keeble's lesson was more personal. He was my writing teacher when I got my graduate degree. When he read my stories he often asked questions I thought at first were stupid. For example, I'd show a character standing in her kitchen, and then walking down the street. John would ask, "How did she get there?"

My voice would take on a slightly weary tone as I patiently explained, "She went through the living room, out the front door, down the steps, across to the gate, and across the sidewalk."

"You didn't tell me that."

"It's obvious."

"Not to readers."

So I'd put it in. Ten pages later, he'd query me about another bumpy or nonexistent transition. It didn't take me long to realize the questions weren't stupid at all, but a great help at forcing me to think critically and precisely about every movement within my manuscript, and to do so from the perspective of a reader, to make logical bridges between every action and the next, every sentence and the next, every argument and the next. Soon, I internalized his asking, and he no longer had to do it.

It doesn't really matter whether we're talking about movies, novels, or polemics (or, for that matter, polemical novels that have been turned into movies), the tracking lesson applies. You want your audience to follow the path you want them to follow (except when you don't), and you want your logic to be clear, smooth, and easy. Except, of course, when you don't.

~

There's only one more lesson of writing I normally give students, which is how to write good dialog. The trick is very simple: don't have people answer each other.

Once again, an example may clarify. Bad dialog: One person asks another, "How are you doing?"

"Not very good."

"Why not?"

"I lost fifty dollars yesterday."

"How?"

"I bet on the Mets."

"You're gambling again, aren't you?" (Left unsaid in this dialog is the fact that betting on the Mets is not normally considered gambling, but rather a charitable contribution to the bookie.)

This dialog is much better: One person asks another, "How are you doing?"

"Goddamn Mets."

"You're gambling again, aren't you?"

This conveys the same information in fewer words. It also uses the adjective *goddamn* to modify the noun *Mets,* which is never a bad thing.

People often talk about wanting their dialog to be realistic, but that is of course the last thing any reader wants, as anyone who has ever processed (and processed, and processed) the end of a best friend's latest romantic relationship could attest: In the three hours a night for three weeks spent doing this, one could have read aloud the entirety of *Anna Karenina.* Even more reasonable conversations would drive readers batty by their repetition. Normally, if you and I talk, you say what you're going to say, then sum it up so you're sure I understand your message. Then I resummarize back to you what you just said so you know I heard you (unless of course I'm in a particularly masculine mood, in which case I ignore what you said except for any one key word that will allow me to change the subject to talk about myself [How's the old joke go? A man and a woman are on a date, and the man says, "I'm tired of talking about me; why don't you talk about me for a while?"], but we'll ignore this possibility for now because we were, after all, talking about dialog and not monolog). After that I give my response to your comments, and then I summarize for you. You summarize my statement, push the conversation forward, summarize your statement, and so on, as the conversation crawls to its eventual destination. This would make unforgivably boring reading. Remember, most movies are shorter than most really good conversations. Even *Shoah* is shorter than some of the best conversations I've had.

The answer to all of this is simple. Take out the summaries, stretch the spaces between the lines. I sometimes liken writing dialog to putting just enough stones in a stream to cross it without getting your feet wet (although why one would object to feeling a stream swirl around one's toes escapes me). If you put the stones too close together, you have to take baby steps, and if you put them too far apart, you fall in. Similarly with your dialog, you want readers neither to have to take baby steps because you made the spaces between comments too small, nor to lose track of what you're saying because you made the spaces too big.

The first dialog exercise I give students is always the same. I ask them to write a story and tell them it can move forward only through dialog: no description allowed (but I still want a scene set, meaning if you want readers to know it takes place on a busy street, you've got to come up with a natural way for one character to say this to another, for example, "These fucking cars, they always make my asthma worse"). You have two characters, one of whom wants to achieve some goal, and will do anything to achieve it. The other does not want that goal to be achieved, and will do anything to prevent it. You can never say explicitly what this goal is, but it must be understood between the two, and clear to readers.

Some of my students at prison have come up with great disagreements. Two people are going to hold up a liquor store; one is sick of always having to be the robber, and wants instead to drive the getaway car. Or two junkies share heroin, but each thinks the other won't give a fair share. A drug dealer wants his beautiful girlfriend to accompany him on his deliveries as eye candy, to boost sales in the highly competitive market ("I used to call for takeout pizza and also call my dealer," a student said, "and the dealer usually got there first"), whereas she feels degraded, but likes the money. Those are often more dramatic than the disagreements chosen by college students, or by people at writing workshops. I remember a woman chose to have a husband and wife disagree over whether he should mow the lawn. That example led me to add another constraint to the assignment: Something desperately important—physical, emotional, or spiritual—must be at stake in this conflict. In her case I suggested that while the conversation itself may be about her attempting to get her husband to cut the grass, their exchange had to be imbued with thirty years of marital friction, so that intead of talking about merely mowing a lawn they're talking about her inability to do anything for herself, and his unwillingness to do anything for her. I asked her to focus all of their frustration on that seemingly simple conversation. She did an excellent job.

But I add more constraints. Only three times, I say, in the entire piece, can either person answer the other directly (as in, "How are you?": "Fine."). They should respond to each other, but not by simply answering questions. Stretch, I say. Further, at least three times in the piece one person has to interrupt, or one person has to begin to say something, only to trail off into . . .

At first, students almost always hate me for this exercise. It's damn hard. But I give them more and more exercises, with more and more people in them ("I want one person to be really stupid, another speaks English as a second tongue, another considers him- or herself to be the brains of the group but is not, a fourth is romantically interested in one of the others, and I want you to make all of this clear in the context of a conflict, without saying any of it directly; and oh, yes, it's hot outside, they hear a dog barking, something stinks, and one of them is late for an engagement; and did I tell you that one of them hasn't cried for thirty years?"), until finally they break through to see how fun and easy dialog is, once they get the trick. Then we get back on speaking terms, although we now no longer answer each other's questions.

I've talked about the rules of writing, but I haven't yet mentioned the first rule of teaching, which is to prepare at least ten times as many discussion questions as you think you'll need. This is not hyperbole.

In this book I've described classroom discussions that went well. I've not talked about the many flops. There are few feelings worse than having used up your last discussion question, which got as little response as the previous six, and looking up at the clock to see you've got an hour and twenty-five minutes left to fill. "Time for in-class writing!"

This leads to another side to the comment I made earlier about my students hungering for meaning. While that's true, it's also true that some class periods were simply dead. And some classes themselves were dead for the entire quarter. I knew early on it wasn't my fault, because during any given quarter I might have one section that talks each night till well after the end of the allotted time and another that finishes the final discussion topic ten minutes after we started.

Normally the classes that wouldn't talk for me still talked at least a little when other students led the class. I think this was partly out of pity: They didn't seem to mind if I sweated it out trying to get them to talk, but they hated to see another student squirming. There was one night, though, that nothing the group leading the class did seemed to work. They'd prepared a series of very provocative questions about God, religion, and students' views on what, if anything, happens after we die. Even more interesting were the group's questions probing the processes by which these opinions had been formed. But the questions didn't matter, because none of the rest of us, except me, answered any of their questions, and I did only after the silence went from awkward to painful, and then from painful to embarrassing. Finally one of the members of the group said, in exasperation, "Don't any of you like to think?"

At last a question someone could, or would, answer. A man said, "No, actually, I don't."

The group member threw a disgusted look back, but before he could say anything, I asked if I could take over. The group was glad to oblige.

I was excited. I said, "There are no judgments in the questions I'm going to ask. I'm just really interested. Defining the act of thinking however you want, how many of you don't like to think?"

About a third of the class raised their hands. It was the third I would have guessed. I say that in no way as a slam against them: It's just that their papers generally contained the least thought.

I was in some ways relieved by this show of hands. It helped me at least slightly to understand something otherwise incomprehensible to me, which is the relative ease with which corporate and governmental propaganda—even transparently stupid propaganda—is propagated and internalized. I keep asking myself whether the politicians and corporate journalists who push this stuff intentionally do evil, or if they just never think on even the most rudimentary level about what they're doing. I also keep asking myself how people repeatedly buy into all this. The show of hands—one-third of college students—at least partly answered this question.

I asked, "What do you do in the shower, or driving, or when you're walking to class?" I didn't think they were practicing no-mind meditation, but I wanted to be sure.

A man said, "I listen to the radio."

A friend of mine calls radio "thought jamming," because the chatter drowns out normal thought.

Someone else said, "I just go over and over how mad I am at my boyfriend."

Another: "I laugh at TV programs from the night before."

Most said, "I don't do anything," or more basically, "I don't know."

I asked one, who likes sports, if he ever thought about football. "No."

"But you watch it all the time."

"So?"

"You don't think about the matchups?"

"No. I just watch."

I have to be honest with you and tell you I don't know what to make of all this. This discussion took place a decade ago, and though I've thought about it often, I still cannot quite wrap my mind around their answers or, especially, the implications.

Until one is committed, there is hesitancy, the chance to draw back, always ineffectiveness. Concerning all acts of initiative and creation, there is one elementary truth, the ignorance of which kills countless ideas and splendid plans: that the moment one definitely commits oneself, then providence moves too. All sorts of things occur to help one that would never otherwise have occurred. A whole stream of events issues from the decision, raising in one's favor all manner of unforeseen incidents and meetings and material assistance, which no man could have dreamed would have come his way. Whatever you do, or dream you can, begin it. Boldness has genius, power and magic in it. Begin it now.

—W. H. Murray

falling in love

I haven't yet told you why I no longer have to force myself to write. It's because I fell in love. Another way to say this is that I fell into something far larger than myself. Yet another way to say this is, well, I'll just tell you the story.

It's the fall of 1987. I'm living in Spirit Lake, Idaho. I'm still counting words, making myself write. For cash, I work with a partner in a small beekeeping woodenware business. It doesn't take much time (though it also doesn't provide much cash), so I read and write a lot. My reading is generally purposeful, as I try to figure out how to write: what works and what doesn't. It's also eclectic, everything from Thomas Mann to Kilgore Trout, Aristotle to Edward Gibbon to Albert Camus to the pulpiest of pulp science fiction, mystery, suspense, and romance to *The 29 Most Common Writing Mistakes and How to Avoid Them*. The stories I write are often modeled on the stories I read, as I try to capture the authors' techniques.

I read a book by James Herriot, one of the *All Things Bright and Beautiful* series about the extraordinarily sappy adventures of a Yorkshire veterinarian. One of the stories is about a man whose only friend is his dog. The dog goes with him daily to a bar. Somehow I know from the first line how the story will end: The dog will die and the man will kill himself. I know also that Herriot is going to use every trick he knows to make me cry. I vow he's not going to get me, and I think I can make it stick since the ending will be no surprise. I get to the end of the story, and when I finally quit crying I get mad at being so easily and obviously manipulated.

Once I'm done being mad I marvel at his skill: How did he make me cry with ink on paper? When I'm done marveling I decide that's a skill I want to have.

I need a plot. Well, I think, if it worked for James Herriot, maybe it will work for me. The story will be about a man whose only friend is his dog. The dog dies, and, because I was a wimp, instead of killing himself the man moves out of town. Since I've never been to Yorkshire, I set it in Nevada, where I lived a few years prior.

For several months I try to write the story, but I can't, mainly because my idea stinks. This makes me unhappy for several reasons, not the least of which is that my words-per-day average is plummeting. At this rate I'll never make it to a million words.

Meanwhile, my woodenware partner's daughter comes up from California. She'd visited the summer before and we'd quickly become close friends. This time, however, isn't a visit. She's seeking refuge from her abusive husband, who's in jail for raping her. We talk a lot about her experience. I share with her the abuse I suffered as a child. But then, and this is a story we've all seen too many times, she drops the charges and starts to think about going back to him. *The beatings weren't that bad,* she says. *Except for this last one, he never hit me in the face. He's going to change; I know that. The problem really isn't him, it's the drugs. My children need a father. How will I support us?*

I talk to her. It does no good. Her father talks to her. Her mother. Nothing. One night I talk to her mother and a family friend until three or four in the morning about what we can do to keep her from going back. We get nowhere. I go home. I sleep.

I awaken at nine that morning with the plot—and much of the early language—for a short story laid out before me. It will be from the perspective of a woman married to an abuser. She becomes good friends with a loner whose only other friend is his dog. Their conversations help her realize she deserves to be treated better than she is. But her husband learns of her friendship, and kills her friend's dog. The friend leaves town. Through that trauma the woman finally learns to love herself enough to give her husband the boot. I think it will take about ten pages— a long story for me at the time—and I vow I won't sleep until it's done. I start to write, and the words come easily, as if I'm dreaming them. But when I get to page six, I realize the story may total fifteen, and I quit for the day. At page twelve, I think it might be twenty. At eighteen, thirty. The dream continues for six months, till I finish a three-hundred-page manuscript.

The book was never published. I sent it to 112 publishers, and received 112 rejections. I know the number because I charted my submissions (I soon came to recognize the appropriateness of the word *submission* in this context) on a paper taped to the wall, then tracked when I got them back and sent them out again: After about 40 rejections I moved the papers to the back of a door where I wouldn't have to see them so often. After about 60, it got so going to the mailbox traumatized me. I wished I had an agent as a buffer, but I got 35 rejections from them, too.

The important thing, though, is that I found the door to where the muse lives, the place where words bubble like water from cold mountain springs. And I was in love. With the words. With the story. With the process. With the feeling of absolute engagement in a struggle that meant something to me.

How did that happen? Part of it, of course, is magic. It's still magic every time it happens, and it happens almost every day now. Part of it is practice, becoming comfortable enough with words and ideas and emotions to be able to shape them with some semblance of clarity and beauty. But there's more. It wasn't simply proficiency. There's a qualitative difference in the experience of writing—and in the words that end up on the paper—

between work written without that engagement and love, and work written with it. There's a click. An opened door. The difference between liking someone and falling in love. When I wrote earlier that the one thing I've learned about writing was how to tell when I'm writing crap, and to stop writing it (I hope the same is true, more broadly, for living as well), I really meant that I can tell when that door is shut, and so when the writing is coming from this side of it. I don't write then. And I can tell when it's open, and then I follow through to the far side, no matter the other circumstances. It could be late, and I have to get up early, but if the door opens, I go through it. I could be driving, in which case I pull over. I could be having sex. (I meant what I said about the best writing being better than sex, but this statement is an oversimplification: The truth is that sex and creativity are tightly tied. Not much is more erotic to me than creativity, and not much is more creative than the erotic. But you knew that already: I'm sure the muse told you, too.)

The question becomes, how/why did the door open, and, most definitely segueing away from sex, how can I help my students to find and open their own doors?

Here's what I know. I cared deeply. I did not want my dear friend to return to her husband. I did not want for her to be hurt. I had a reason to write. I was trying to communicate. I wasn't writing to raise my word count. Nor was I writing precisely to get published (which is a good thing, since the novel never was). Nor was I writing as practice. I was desperately trying to convey a message—an experience—to my friend. It was like Charles Johnson said: This is what I would write if someone were going to kill me after I wrote the last word. The same holds true for every book I've written.

This ties back to everything I've been talking about. How do I help my students uncover their passion? What infuriates or terrifies or enraptures them? What does all three, and more? What messages do my students desperately want and need to convey, and to whom must they convey them? How can I help them trigger passions strong enough that they lose self-consciousness and fall completely into the feelings, the words, the messages?

It goes back to the same old questions, but with a new one at the end. Who are you? What do you love? And the new one: What do you want?

If you tell me who you are, tell me what you love, tell me what you want, I'll tell you what you should probably be writing. Or maybe I won't have to. You will already have started.

On your own, you have to face the responsibility for how you spend time. But in school you don't. What they make you do may obviously be a waste but at least the responsibility isn't charged to your account. School in this respect is, once again, like the army or jail. Once you're in, you may have all kinds of problems but freedom isn't one of them.

—Jerry Farber

revolution

Last week, a friend sent me a couple of e-mails detailing her views on education. The first read, "Having been spared the public school system until fourth grade, I never, from day one, bought it. They didn't get me early enough. I can remember that first day, my absolute horror that this was where my playmates had been coming day after day for years. Why had no one told me it was day prison? I was even more horrified as the realization set in that I, too, had now been sentenced to this hell for the next eight years. I still feel very strongly that my having been spared those early years of indoctrination has always been one of my greatest strengths." And the next: "I had a few teachers who cut me slack for my creative approaches to getting by, those who were allies in getting through the miserable bullshit we all had to endure, but never one who loved me into becoming myself. They were all still so damaged from their own debilitating institutional education that few could even see the possibility of what real education is. My trust has been violated so many times by that system that I've grown to really hate it. Of course, I'm grateful to know I hate it. And the way I've always known it was fucked was that I actually had that point of reference of true education early on at the hands of my mother. I loved being homeschooled. There was no stress around learning. It was play. All children (and other humans, and for that matter nonhumans!) love to learn. You really have to work hard to beat that out of them. And the system amazingly is able to do it in a very few years. And I never pretend I don't hate it, or that I think it can be reformed—it's another thing (actually it's not another thing, it's the same thing) that just needs to come down in its entirety. I'm continually amazed and horrified at how seemingly bright, intelligent parents do this incredible job at home with their little ones, so careful about their care providers and diet and media exposure, and then just hand them over to the system at five years old. It's this huge blindspot. And the justifications are equally amazing. I liken it to the phenomenon with which I'm sure you're familiar, of parents who deliver their children to the hands of their abuser. This morning I went with a friend to take her son to school (first grade) and when we were walking back out she said she'd seen a lot of mothers crying last week dropping their children off to their first year in school. She kind of smiled and gave me this 'all us mothers know that pain' sort of look. I said, 'I bet,' and, 'Why do you think all those mothers cry?' She didn't answer. She knows, I think, it's because they're all over-riding every instinct they have for their child's well-being."

This all leads to the question I've been so carefully avoiding throughout this book. It has to do with whether we should attempt to work within our rotten system, or whether we should try to tear the whole thing down.

By coincidence, I received another e-mail today, this one from another friend, also about education. She wrote: "It's important to look at education because it's a relationship we're all forced to enter, and because it can be seen as a metaphor or template for all of our other relationships of domination. I've been thinking about this a lot lately because for the last two years I've been sitting in two seats, in the role of victim (Ph.D. student) and perpetrator (teacher), and I've realized that when we talk about education (or the culture) we're really talking about undoing a relationship of domination. Every day I struggle to find ways to not be oppressed (not possible really) and not to oppress (challenging, and I'm not sure how successful I am). On the classroom level, I've tried to not perpetrate emotional violence or coercion on my students, which has caused me to butt my head time and again against this question: What is the difference between leadership and coercion? When I try to empower my students, I sometimes succeed and sometimes fail. Especially in my smaller classes I can be most myself and teach the way I believe. I can make the classes real, and the students love learning about themselves. But I've found that many of my students in the larger classes are often rude to me unless I Exert Some Authority. Some of these students read my openness as weakness and my gentleness as vulnerability. When openness and gentleness inspire hate and ridicule where do we go from here? So many students expect me to 'lead' as they have been led before, and they certainly have ways of making that happen. It reminds me of a relationship I was in long ago in which my lover pushed at me emotionally over a period of months, then physically cornered me. I yelled for him to get the hell out, and I will never forget the look on his face: He was smug, seemingly happy, his expression telling me he'd finally maneuvered me into acting the way he wanted me to act. I left the relationship. Or I guess it would be more accurate to say I left the enforced pattern of relations. This sort of thing happens all the time. The system of domination permeates every aspect of all of our relationships, and there are mechanisms that trigger its reenactment in all parts of our lives. When that system of relations enters even our most sacred of relationships, the relationships of the body and the heart, it need do no more. But of course it doesn't stop there. The question becomes: How do we enact relationships that are not coercive in a system that does not support that? It's very complex. I know my students are rebelling against their own experience of oppression, but I get the brunt of it. And there are students who have been so wounded by parents, teachers, and other authority figures that no matter what I do I can't reach them because they can't hear me. What do I do about them? For example, one of my rudest students gave a great speech at the end of last year, about research on the emotional abuse of children and how it feels. I hadn't reached him in my class—he'd been rude throughout—and suddenly I understood why. And I was sorry. I guess this is all a way of coming around to three questions: (1) Is material that comes out of the white supremacist, capitalist, patriarchy worth teaching? (2) I know that the purpose of real education is to allow people to learn about themselves and the larger world, but what then substantively is worth learning? and (3) How can this system work?"

I don't know answers to her questions. Here is what I do know: I hate industrial civilization, for what it does to the planet, for what it does to communities, for what it does to individual nonhumans (both wild and domesticated), and for what it does to individual humans (both wild and domesticated). I hate the wage economy, because it causes—forces is probably more accurate—people to sell their lives doing things they do not love, and because it rewards people for harming each other and destroying their landbases. I hate industrial schooling because it commits one of the only unforgivable sins there is: It leads people away from themselves, training them to be workers and convincing them it's in their best interest to be ever more loyal slaves, rowing the galley that *is* industrial civilization ever more fervently—enthusiastically, orgiastically—to hell, compelling them to take everything and everyone they encounter down with them. And I participate in this process. I help make school a little more palatable, a little more fun, as students are trained to do their part in the ongoing destruction of the planet, as they enter the final phases of trading away their birthright as the free and happy humans they were born to be for their roles as cogs in the giant industrial machine, or worse, as overseers of the giant factory/enslavement camp we once recognized as a living earth. Doesn't that make me, in essence, a collaborator? Hell, drop the *in essence.*

Robert Jay Lifton, probably the world's foremost authority on the psychology of genocide, made clear in his crucial book *The Nazi Doctors* that many of the physicians working at concentration camps such as Auschwitz attempted to make life as comfortable as they could for their charges, doing everything in their power to save inmates' lives, except the most important thing of all: questioning the Auschwitz reality, that is, the atrocity-inducing superstructure under which they operated (often without anesthetic). The fact that industrial education murders souls instead of bodies doesn't reduce my culpability. And I must also recognize my culpability not only for participating in the larger processes that destroy or deform the humanity of students (it's as though I'm putting soft cushions on the benches of the galley so the slaves don't hurt their poor bums) but also for participating in the larger processes that train the overseers: As much as I may wish to pretend I'm helping to take down civilization, when I teach at a university I'm actively training the future technocrats who will prop up civilization and who, by simply doing their jobs as well and perhaps as good-heartedly as I do mine, will commit genocide the world over and eviscerate what still remains of the natural world. As Raul Hilberg described so aptly in his monumental *The Destruction of the European Jews,* the vast majority of the perpetrators of the Holocaust neither shot nor gassed their victims: They wrote memos, answered telephones, went to meetings. They did their own little jobs in larger bureaucracies that did not have as their function anything so indelicate as mass murder, but rather were merely maximizing production and minimizing cost at factories (left unsaid: by using slave labor); freeing up land and other properties necessary for the economy's full functioning (left unsaid: by invading eastern Europe and the Soviet Union); protecting homeland security (left unsaid: by imprisoning or killing those considered threats, including Jews, Romani, homosexuals, dissidents, the "work-shy" [that is, those unwilling to get a job, or, as SS Oberführer Greifelt stated, "persons who were unwilling to participate in the working life of the nation and who were merely scraping by as work-shy . . . had to be dealt with by coercive means and set to work," which in this case meant they were sent to Buchenwald]), and so on; and gathering clothes, eyeglasses, shoes, and gold for use by good Germans (left unsaid: the source of these materials).

To be clear, and to make certain neither you nor I are able to let ourselves off the hook: Industrial civilization is killing the planet, and we're all doing our parts. It couldn't do so without our contributions, whether we're geophysical engineers exploring for natural gas in the Utah desert, advertisers writing copy for Ford Motor Company, flight attendants handing out peanuts on transcontinental trips, physicians keeping workers and executives more or less healthy, psychologists keeping consumers more or less functioning, writers creating books for people to read in their spare time, or teachers helping these writers to never bore their readers. This deathly system needs us all.

Teaching at the prison brings this question into even sharper focus. Every time I walk through the gates I'm helping to support the largest prison system in the world, and also the most racist, one that imprisons black people at a higher rate even than South Africa did during apartheid. But at the same time, I know that many of my students have told me explicitly and repeatedly that our classes are the only things they look forward to all week, the only things that keep them sane.

I've been stuck on this question of reform versus revolution for years now, and perhaps it's time I finally took my own advice and realized I'm asking the wrong question. Reform versus revolution is a false dichotomy. The first answer is that we need both: Without a revolution the planet is dead, but if we simply wait for the revolution the planet will still be dead before the revolution comes. For years I and hundreds of other activists around the country filed what are called timber sale appeals in an (ultimately unsuccessful) attempt to get the Forest Service to stop putting out illegal, fiscally irresponsible, and environmentally destructive timber sales on public lands. Now, I oppose all industrial forestry, and especially oppose all industrial forestry on public lands. Further, I know that the administrative and judicial systems are rigged in favor of corporations. (Why mince words: They are rigged in favor of the destruction of the planet's life-support systems.) But none of this stopped me from temporarily using that reformist tactic. Anything to try to save the forests. Which leads to the second answer, which is that morality is always circumstantial. You do what is right from the place you are, and you attempt to put yourself in places where you can do the right thing, or rather things, because temperament and abilities also help determine what a person should do.

I can hear the voices now, saying again and again: *slippery slope, slippery slope. Remember the doctors at Auschwitz?* But *every* slope is slippery. So what? Part of my birthright as a moral and sentient being is that I get to make moral judgments. It's my duty and joy to confront these acts of discernment as honestly and open-mindedly as I can. And then even moreso. And moreso than that. The key component in the Nazi doctors despicable behavior was their failure to question the Auschwitz reality. And frankly, the vast majority of us just as despicably fail to question industrial civilization, the wage economy, and, right to the point of this discussion, industrial education. Constantly questioning one's context, whether that context is Auschwitz, Disney, Pelican Bay State Prison, industrial civilization, Eastern Washington University, or the Great Glorious Luddite Revolution is to hook up to the strongest safety line I know against sliding down any slippery slope. Because these slopes are most dangerous, I think, when unexamined.

~

About week seven of every quarter I ask myself the same question: What would we talk about if I had the same students two consecutive quarters, or even two semesters?

And nearly every quarter I come up with the same answer. If this first quarter is about liberation, the second would be about responsibility. Every person needs to learn and experience—incorporate, take into the body—both. And they're inseparable. Either without the other becomes a parody, and leads to inappropriate, destructive, and self-destructive behaviors generally characteristic of unconscious or unintentional parodies. Responsibility without freedom is slavery. As we see. Freedom without responsibility is immaturity. As we also see. Put them together and you've got an entire culture consisting of immature slaves. As we see as well, unfortunately both for us and for those we meet. These parodies may be very good if you're interested in growing the economy, but they're very bad if you're interested in life.

This question of pursuing liberation and responsibility in the classroom hasn't come up at the prison, because the life circumstances of my students there are different, meaning what they need and what they can ask from me is different. And what I am allowed to give them is different. The classes, some of which have run for several years now, are more technical. Of course I still cheerlead, but we don't play capture the flag or hide-and-go-seek. And it somehow seems inappropriate to do the most important writing exercise—the finger exercise—or to throw chairs or chalk while a gunner walks a catwalk overhead, as is the case in one of the classes. My work in the classrooms at the prison is a bit more circumscribed, a bit less philosophical.

Really, though, the differences are superficial, and, as always, contextual. The foundation remains the same for both college and prison, which is to respect and love my students into becoming who they are.

~

It's week eight at the university, and there's revolution in the air. Many of the students are upset at me. One says, "You talk about liberation, about how we're the real bosses in the classroom, how you want us to take charge of our own learning. But that's all crap. You still take roll."

Another: "You say you don't want to grade us, but check marks are still coercion."

Another: "What if I don't want to write anything?"

"Then I guess you'll flunk," I say.

She responds, "I used to think you're better than other teachers, but you're all the same. You just smile when you push us around. Even worse, you get *us* to smile when you push us around."

I'm happy. They get it. Everything in this class has been aiming toward this moment, this rejection on their part of my authority. This is the point. I want to chuck the check marks and give them all 4.0s. I want to chuck the 4.0s and not give them anything except what I've already given them, which is time and acceptance. But I don't let on I'm happy. I argue with them. Not much, but a little. And then I concede their points.

The one who used to think me better than other teachers says, "I don't blame you. I like you. You're great. But you're trying to fit yourself—and fit all this acceptance and all this teaching us to care about ourselves—into this whole other system based on coercion, and that's just ridiculous."

A slightly pained look masks my joy. I ask, "What should I do, then? Do you want me to change the way I teach? Do you want me to do the whole grade thing?"

"No," she says, horrified.

"What, then?"

"Change the whole system."

"How do I do that?"

She thinks a while, then says the best thing possible: "You're smart. You need to figure that out on your own. I've got enough trouble trying to deal with this in my own life."

I love doing this work.

~

Just this weekend I taught at a writers' conference. It was fun. The only problem was that it took place in a junior high. I hadn't walked those types of halls, heard that particular squeak of my sneakers on the smooth floors, for many years. More to the point, I hadn't been forced to enter one of those classrooms. Things are far worse in there even than I remember. One of the first things I noticed when I walked into the room where my workshops were to be held was a bright red bumper sticker stuck to the front of the teacher's desk: "This is not Burger King, and you can't have it your way." Signs (some handwritten in magic marker, some mass-produced) are posted all over the walls—and I mean *all* over the walls—telling students that if they misbehave they'll be sent to the principal's office. One orders, in all caps, that STUDENTS

MUST NEVER SPEAK WITHOUT RAISING THEIR HANDS AND BEING GIVEN PERMISSION BY THE TEACHER.

Although it was a math classroom, it was clear that the real point was, as always, submission to authority. I don't know how I survived it. I don't know how any children survive it. I guess the truth is that in a very real sense many don't. And *that* is the point.

Deep root, lofty trunk, dense foliage: from the center of the world rises a thornless tree, one of those trees that knows how to give themselves to the birds. Around the tree whirl dancing couples, navel to navel, undulating to a music that wakens stones and sets fire to ice. As they dance, they dress and undress the tree with streaming ribbons of every color. . . . The tree of life knows that, whatever happens, the warm music spinning around it will never stop. However much death may come, however much blood may flow, the music will dance men and women as long as the air breathes them and the land plows and loves them.

—Eduardo Galeano

walking on water

I t's the third-to-last week of class at the university, and I bring in a documentary about the Names Project, also known as the AIDS Quilt. The film tells stories of a few of those who've died and been memorialized by panels in the quilt, and of the making of those panels by people who loved them. When I turn on the lights in the room afterward, I see that even many of the football players in the class have their heads down, and when they bring them up their shoulders are tight, eyes red.

"If you were to die," I begin, "how would you be remembered?"

I pause.

No one says anything.

I start again, "Or rather, *when* you die—because it's not *if* but *when*—what will people say about you?"

They're quiet. Most are thinking.

"I've got an assignment for you. I want you to design your AIDS Quilt panel. You don't have to sew it. Just put it on construction paper or something."

Still silence in the room, until a young man blurts out, "I'm not going to do it. I'm not going to die of some gay disease."

He's been a homophobe (and misogynist) all quarter, so his response doesn't surprise me. I've got an answer for him. Because the documentary pointed out that heterosexuals have died as well, I don't need to make that statement again. I say, "Your panel can be for another quilt. A very special quilt. This will be for those who were in a car, drinking alcohol and having sex with four women all at the same time, and who got in an accident. The women survived. You died."

He doesn't seem to have a problem with the scenario.

"One more thing," I say to the class. "You can do this exercise yourself, but it's even better if you get someone who loves you to do it for you. A parent, sibling, lover, friend."

Someone asks, "You mean we get credit for someone else doing our work?"

"What a deal," I respond.

They bring in their panels over the next week, and they talk about them. Most have been designed by others, nearly all have been put together with great care: very few have been done just for credit. The son of a farm family brings in construction paper covered with bags of soil and seeds. A volleyball player's panel has laces from her tennis shoes, along with pictures of her parents and a ticket stub from *Les Misérables*. Another student's has strands of hair from her children and a reed from her clarinet. A few bring in panels not of construction paper, but actual quilt pieces that either they or their mothers have made. My mother designs mine. She includes a bookmark on which she's count-stitched a quill pen, representing my writing; a couple of track spikes, representing my love of sports; a photograph of my dogs; a little piece of honeycomb, for my years as a beekeeper; and a drawing of salmon rushing through a broken dam.

The real point of this exercise is, as is often the case, something different than what's on the surface. The point isn't so much to get them to think about their own mortality, nor to piece together an answer to that same old question I ask all quarter—*Who are you?*—nor for them to have fun, nor even to make us more intimate as a class, although I'm glad each of these takes place. The real point is to give them the opportunity to have people who care about them express that affection by attending to them, by mirroring back to them the traits they most cherish.

~

It's nearing the end of the quarter. Today in class we're going to take polls. When I was in college, I heard rumors of people who studied so much they only slept two hours per night: I never believed them. In fact I disbelieved them enough that for a couple of years I kept track on graph paper what time I went to bed and how much I slept (one year I didn't get to bed before midnight until after August 1), as well as how many hours per day I studied, and for what classes. It was pretty interesting. I still have the sheets. I also heard rumors of those who got drunk several times per week; most of my friends didn't drink. I thought that other people, too, might be interested in what exactly is normal— by which I do not mean normalized or considered morally proper, but what is common—and so I'd asked students a couple of days previous to think of questions to ask the class. They brought them in on scraps of paper.

Interestingly, we all—myself included—shy away from questions directly about sex, probably because we all sense that could be embarrassing for those who perceive themselves too far from the norm, as having started sex too early or too late (or not yet), as having too few or too many partners. We also know that the young couple would lie on their answers to those questions, anyway, so it's probably best we just don't ask. We also have an explicit rule that no judgments or even attempts at persuasion are allowed. The point of all this questioning is not to be right but to simply find out what people feel. That said, students are encouraged to tell stories that might illuminate their answers.

I pick a paper from the scrap pile in front of me.

How many hours do you sleep a night?

My students average probably six and a half, with a low of four and a high of eleven.

If you didn't have to worry about a schedule, how many hours—and what hours—would you sleep?

When I ask this question, dreamy looks come over their faces, as rapturous as when I set up the fantasy of meeting the person at the conference. The notion of sleeping as long as they want feels good enough that it takes a while for them even to answer. They'd sleep a lot more, they'd pound their alarm clocks into unidentifiable bits, and they'd sleep at all hours, day or night.

How many of you don't drink alcohol at all, or at most one or two glasses of wine a year with family?

Probably a quarter of the class.

How many of you get drunk at least once a month?

Going on half.

Once a week?

A quarter of the class.

Excluding books read for school, how many of you read a book a week?

Two or three.

A month?

A quarter.

Less than one a year?

Two or three.

Did you ever cheat in high school?

Everyone except two women, one American and one Chinese, says *yes*.

Have you cheated in college?

After a few nervous laughs, about half cop to it. I ask those who say yes to state their names clearly into a button on my shirt.

They ask if I cheated.

"Depends on how you define cheating," I say.

They're not buying it.

"I copied homework from willing friends all the time, and allowed them to copy mine. That never felt like cheating to me. That was a political statement, a rejection of the competitive attitudes that undergird our culture, a statement of solidarity with my fellow students, a movement toward a more cooperative model of education."

They still don't buy it.

"I probably shouldn't tell you this, but I recycled a few old high school papers in college classes. But that was done for purely educational purposes. I wanted to see the difference in how papers were graded in high school versus college. Papers that got me an A in high school got a B in college. I think that's important information, and I was willing to sacrifice writing those papers just so I could gain that information and pass it on to you now."

They don't buy this either.

"But there were two times I cheated on tests. I had a minerology lab fall semester my freshman year, where each week they passed around numbered rocks we were supposed to identify. Well, as each person passed his rock, he slid his paper, too, so the next person could see it. At first I was shocked and horrified by the commonplace nature of this cheating, and then around Thanksgiving I was even more shocked and horrified to find that with no discernible transition on my part I'd joined in. I learned a far more important lesson than rock identification, which is that no matter how much something might stink at first, eventually you get used to the stench and it doesn't bother you anymore. That stench could be anything from cheating to grades to civilization itself."

Someone says, "You said there was another time you cheated."

"I was taking a multiple-choice chemistry exam, also my

freshman year, in one of those big lecture halls. I was near the back. I was having trouble with one particular question—actually I was having trouble with lots of questions, but I happened to be working on number twenty-seven—and had just taken my best guess on it. I glanced up at the clock, and I swear the guy in front of me was holding his paper in the air right in line with my vision. And he had just finished question twenty-seven! I couldn't believe it! It was a sign from the gods. So I changed my answer to his. Of course when I got the results back, my original answer was right. That pretty much cured me of copying off other people. I haven't done it since."

I tell them there's one more thing I need to say about cheating, something I wish I had known when I was in school: The instructor can see almost everything that goes on in the classroom. If you think you're sneaking a magazine inside your textbook in some class, the truth is that the instructor either doesn't care or is too tired to tell you to stop. "Had I known that," I say, "I would have been a lot more careful."

This brings up another question: How many of you cheated in this class?

"How would we cheat," a woman asks, almost batting her eyelashes, "when there's a check-mark system?"

I point to the recycling bin.

"Oh, I never thought of that!" The eyelashes really are batting now.

Everyone laughs. Probably half of them acknowledge recycling a paper or two. I don't care. I asked them to write a tremendous amount through the quarter, five to ten times as much as students in other "Principles of Thinking and Writing" classes (who had to write a total of three, count 'em, three, papers), and so for the most part I didn't mind them reusing an old paper or two, as long as it didn't get out of hand. In fact, I had several people turn in papers or stories they'd written previously specifically to take advantage of my editorial attentions and take them to doneness. I had no problem with that at all. There had, however, been two papers I did object to. One had been turned in with a previous instructor's comments simply whited out. The other had not been merely recycled but written by someone else: A foreign student who normally couldn't construct even a simple sentence in English was suddenly describing the "laser-like precision of the surgeon's steady hand."

I pick up another scrap of paper. If you see a policeman, and you're not doing anything illegal, nor do you *need* a cop, on a scale of minus five ("fucking pig") to plus five ("Thank you, Baby Jesus"), what is your instant feeling?

The average is about minus three. Even the deputy's response is below zero.

"What if you see a member of the parking patrol?"

The score is a perfect negative five. People begin throwing out fantasies of what they'd like to do to these people that shock even the most gothic classmembers.

Next question. If you're a woman, do you shave your legs and armpits? If you're a man, would you date someone who didn't shave her legs and armpits?

First, I tell them I object to the sexist specificity of these questions, and say we also need to ask men if they shave their legs and armpits, and to ask women the complementary question. No men shave. Surprisingly (at least to me) only one woman doesn't shave. Many women wave their arms and slide around in their chairs saying, "Oh, gross. I could never go hairy." It's clear they're not judging the woman who does—and she's clear on this, too—but instead manifesting the heebie-jeebies that for whatever reason their own body hair gives them. I'm the only man in the room who doesn't care whether a partner shaves. "By the time it gets to the point where I even find that out," I say, "I've already formed a pretty strong opinion of the person."

Do you believe in God?

Before we can answer this, we have to create a series of definitions. Does God mean a Big Guy with a White Beard? Is God a process? Does god have a small *g*? Are there multiple gods? We end up with the following categories (and many people agreed with multiple possibilities): monotheist (including Christian, Jewish, Muslim, and so on), half the class; god as a name we project onto the mysterious processes of life (including those things we consider nonliving), half the class; pantheism (god in everything), a third; polytheism (many gods, including the possibility of some of the religions from the Indian subcontinent), four or five people; atheist, three or four; agnostic, two or three.

They ask what I think, and I tell them a story. I had just gotten on a plane when it was announced that there were mechanical problems, and we had to switch to a different one. On the new plane, I now sat next to a large man who was reading his Bible. When flight attendants walked by, he dropped slips of paper with Biblical quotes into their pockets. I tried to hold the book I was reading slightly between us, hoping it would act as a shield to keep him away. It didn't. He kept "accidentally" jostling me, then apologizing, clearly waiting to use my acknowledgment of his apology as a foot in the door toward saving my soul. When that didn't work, he finally grasped my knee and asked, earnestly, "Do you know why God made a mechanical error on the other plane? It was so the seating could be rearranged. And do you know why He did that?"

I had an answer: "Yes, so I can tell you all about pantheism."

He leaned away, and now he was the one using a book—the Bible—as a shield. It was a much shorter trip than it would otherwise have been.

Another question: Are there swear words you won't say?

Two people simultaneously say the obvious: "Fuck no."

We make a list. I'm slightly surprised. More people won't say *goddamn* than won't say *fuck*. Most of those who won't say *goddamn* will say either word by itself, but never together. I'm also slightly surprised that the fundamentalist woman gets into the spirit of this question. (She had trouble with the question about beliefs in a deity: When an American Indian started to explain his spiritual practices, she said, "Oh, you Indians believe in ghosts, don't you?" He paused a moment, then just said, "I guess you could say that.") She doesn't use any swear words (including gosh or darn), but she doesn't mind other people mentioning words they will or won't use. The word that most people find most offensive is, to no one's surprise, *cunt*. Even when I start to ask the question, some women squirm as feverishly as they had about the possibility of not shaving their legs. One covers her ears and squeals.

I had told my supervisor I was going to ask this question, and his response says more about our relationship than any other story I could tell. He frowned, then said, mock-earnestly, "How many times do I have to tell you, Derrick, never to say anything worse than *motherfucker* in class?"

I ask the class: Are you happy?

Most are not. Some don't even know what that would look (much less feel) like.

Do you think you'll ever be happy?

Most say no.

Do you think we live in a democracy?

They laugh. Of course not.

Do you think the government better serves corporations or human beings?

They laugh again. Of course corporations.

Do you think the world will be a better place in twenty years?

No.

Forty?

No.

A hundred?

No.

What do you think it would take for you to be happy? What do you think it would take for the world to be a better place?

They don't know.

~

It's the first day of the next-to-last week. I say, "I have one final assignment for you."

They wait.

"I want you to walk on water."

They still wait. They have no idea what I'm talking about.

"Ready to get on with today's class discussion?"

"No—" one says.

Another says, "But—"

"Oh, yes, of course," I say. "There's one other thing. Afterwards I want you to write about it. Sorry for the confusion."

Somebody says, "I don't get it."

I answer, "You will."

The same fellow as always says, "But what's the point of us doing this?"

"You'll get that, too."

I try to get on with class, but they won't let me. They keep asking what I want them to do. I keep answering the same way: I want you to walk on water, and then write about it.

Finally, a woman loses patience, and says to the class, "Everybody here knows the story of Jesus walking on water, right? What's the story about? It's about someone doing something impossible."

One of the more literal-minded students responds, "But if it's impossible, we can't do it."

"That's the point," the woman responds. "He wants you to do the impossible."

"But—"

"That word—*but*—is why you can't," she says, manifesting the trick of good dialog.

"Only Jesus could walk on water," says the Christian.

"That's not even good theology, much less psychology," says the woman. "The others could, too, so long as they didn't doubt they could. So long as they didn't get self-conscious—"

"So long as they kept looking at Jesus," countered the Christian.

"Forget Jesus."

"That's blasphemy!"

"I'm not a Christian, so that word doesn't scare me. The metaphor of the story is that once you look inside and figure out who you are (and once you begin to believe in your abilities) you find yourself able to produce—create—amazing possibilities you previously couldn't even imagine. Like walking on water." She looks at me: "Is that about right?"

I nod, and say, slowly, "I think—"

She cuts me off, "It's even better, because once you get to that place where you can walk on water, you suddenly find yourself on solid ground where before you thought there was no support. And this support comes not from you, but from everything around you. Once you begin to act from this place, the whole universe conspires to support you." She looks back at me, pauses.

I say again, "I think—"

But again she's off and running, "And that's really what we need. The whole system is fucked. Everything is fucked. The planet's being killed. We're going into these awful fucking jobs we all hate, and what's required of each of us individually and all of us collectively is a miracle, or a million miracles. And that's what Derrick's asking of us, to go out and commit some miracles, and then write about them. That's not too much to ask, is it?"

I say, "I take it you've thought about this topic a little bit."

"Just a little bit," she says.

~

The papers come in. They're good. A few people—members of the Literal-Minded Club—put an inch of water into bathtubs and take a step across that. A couple more cross frozen ponds.

But many students accomplish miracles. Not of the parlor-trick variety, accomplished with the aid of quick hands and misdirection; nor Godlike miracles in which we can safely disbelieve because of our notion that some great God lives in heaven and that no great and small hosts of gods and goddesses live on earth; nor the miracles that surround us and which no one has to accomplish—the inspiration and expiration of every breath, the formation of fog and its condensation on the tips of leaves, the stripes of black and brown on the back of a ground squirrel, its quick movement, its conversion into food for other creatures after its death, love. Instead the miracles they accomplish are no less than these because they are simple acts of courage and of stepping away from who they thought they were before—and who they *were* before—and into who they are now. One woman ends an abusive relationship. Another acknowledges her bulimia and seeks help. A very shy woman asks a man out on a date: He says yes. A Japanese man tells his parents he doesn't want to be an accountant, but instead an artist. Another man says that all of his writing that quarter counts as walking on water; writing had always before terrified him, but no longer is that true. Another says the same about thinking.

The people in my class, including me, do not need to be taught. We need simply to be encouraged, to be given heart, to be allowed to grow into our own large hearts. We do not need to be governed by external schedules—by the ticking of the ubiquitous classroom clock—nor told what and when we need to learn, nor what we need to express, but instead we need to be given time, not as a constraint, but as a gift in a supportive place where we can explore what we want and who we are, with the assistance of others who care about us also. This is true not only for me and for my students, but for all of us, including our nonhuman neighbors. We all so want to love and be loved, accept and be accepted, cherished, and celebrated simply for being who we are. And that is not so very difficult.

~

A woman comes in to talk about one of her papers. It is a farewell letter to her best friend, who is moving cross-country. The letter is solid. She reads it to me out loud. I don't say very much. When she finishes, I ask, "How do you feel about her leaving?"

She starts to cry, then to sob. She can't talk.

When she slows down, I say, "Put that on paper."

"You mean we can put our emotions in our papers like that?"

I smile.

~

She comes back the next day, with a new letter. She begins to read, and stops, because the words move her too much. She gives the letter to me. I begin to read. I, too, have to stop. When I can again speak, I say, "This is good. This is really good."

"I get it," she says.

It is the last day. I've thought a long time about what ending we could give the class that will sufficiently honor what we've shared. I'm there when the students come in. We chat till it's time to start. I stand, walk to the chalkboard, pick up some chalk, make as if I'll throw it at the back wall, then stop. They laugh. I begin to write, just words and phrases, of some of the things we've shared or accomplished. A barbecue one group hosted in a park just off school grounds, bringing hamburgers, hot dogs, and gardenburgers for the vegetarians. The night I showed the film *Koyaanisqatsi.* The night I showed *One Flew over the Cuckoo's Nest,* and the next class period when we talked about the importance of McMurphy's unsuccessful attempt to lift the impossibly heavy, marble-sided watering station that Chief later uses to escape the institution, and McMurphy's famous line: "But I tried, didn't I? Goddamn it. At least I did that."

Someone now asks, "Is that an example of walking on water?"

I respond, "It got someone out of the institution."

Someone calls out, "The first rule of writing."

I write it on the board.

Someone else yells, "Let the kid out of the closet." I whirl and this time throw the chalk. I get more, and throw that. Then I write down what she said.

"The time you had us write about the thing we've done in our lives we're the most proud of."

"The night the Asian students tried to teach us to use chopsticks by picking up tiny beans."

A man says, "I'm not sure whether they were teaching us or laughing at our incompetence."

"And the time we tried to get Derrick to do the moonwalk."

Tried is the key word.

"Blindfolded soccer."

"The Annoying Child!"

"Ranch dressing!"

"The bullet."

"The night we wrote ghost stories."

"S'mores."

"Oh, my God! Do you remember the chocolate chip cookies?"

I'm writing as fast as I can. I cover board after board, moving from the front of the room to the site of the Great Chalkboard War to the back. Still they keep calling out. Time is running down.

The man who asked this so often asks, "What's the point?"

I write that down.

He says, "No, what's the point of what you're doing right now?"

I turn to him. I don't know what to say.

Suddenly the woman who wrote the farewell letter to her friend slams her hand down on her desk. She cries out, "I get it. The point is that he can't tell us the point. The point is that we have to get it ourselves."

I walk to the empty desk next to hers. I sit. I place the chalk on her desk. I say, quietly, yet loud enough that all can hear, "There's nothing else I can teach you. Good luck. Have fun."

~

The tragedy of industrial schooling is made all the worse by the promise of education, the promise of drawing us out, leading us forth. As midwives attending to the births of their students, teachers carry an awesome responsibility with correspondingly awesome possibilities. Education, if it is to be worthy of its true meaning, can, should, and must be at the forefront of resistance to the routine dehumanization of our whole industrialized mass culture. That is possible. I have done it. So have others. But it is rare. Too many teachers, like too many students, too many workers at too many war manufacturing plants, too many writers, too many politicians, too many people who could be human beings but who have been trained by their schooling and by their work and by their pursuit of money and their pursuit of acceptance and by their very real fear of being who they are step away from this responsibility, and in so doing lead themselves and those around them ever farther from their hearts, and lead us all ever closer to the personal and planetary annihilation that is the looming end point of industrial civilization.

If one of the most unforgivable sins is to lead people away from themselves, we must not forgive the processes of industrial education.

There is, however, an alternative. Or rather, there are as many alternatives as there are people, and most especially as there are people engaged in active, thoughtful relationships with their communities, which includes their living landbases, the land where they live, the land that supports and nourishes them.

I've heard it said that within our deathly culture, the most revolutionary thing anyone can do is follow one's heart. I would add that once you've begun to do that—to follow your own heart—the most moral and revolutionary thing you can do is help others find *their* hearts, to find themselves. It's much easier than it seems.

Time is short. It's short for our planet—the planet that is our home—that is being killed while we stand by. And it is even shorter for all of those students whose lives are slipping away from them with every awful tick of the clock on the classroom wall.

There is much work to be done. What are you waiting for? It's time to begin.

acknowledgments

First, I would like to thank my students at Eastern and Pelican Bay for being who they are, and for all they taught me. It was an honor and a joy to work with them.

I am deeply grateful to Dana Elder, who was the best supervisor anyone could ever dream of, and a damn good friend to boot. He taught me more than I will ever be able to fully appreciate.

Helen Whybrow, Cannon Labrie, Eliza Thomas, Collette Fugere, and Margo Baldwin helped form this book and bring it to print. Thank you.

I am grateful to Deda Bea, Bridget Kinsella, Laurel Luddite, Teelyn Mauney, Tiiu Ruben, and Jen Sweigert for their thoughts on education.

I am thankful to and for my mother, Mary Jensen, who taught me how to think, how to question and never stop asking questions (with the way she encourages questioning and thinking, I can only imagine the Annoying Child routines I put her through), and how to respect and accept myself and others. She is the most accepting person I've ever met.

Words cannot express the depth of my gratitude to my muse, whose words, ideas, emotions never fail. I love working with you. You are my bones, my flesh. I cannot imagine life without you.

As always, my deepest debt is to the land where I have lived. I carry with me lessons from the irrigation ditch in Colorado, the river in Nevada, the forests in Idaho, Washington, and California, and all the creatures who live in these places and who have taught me how to be human.

bibliography

Abbey, Edward. Desert Solitaire: A Season in the Wilderness. New York: Ballantine, 1968. So far as I'm concerned, there's no doubt about it: Abbey's best book. Stunning.

Abbot, Edwin A. Flatland: A Romance of Many Dimensions. 1884. Reprint, New York: Dover Publications, 1992. This is a mind-blowing little book. Emphasis on mind-blowing. Secondary emphasis on little. And it's only a dollar fifty, so there's really no excuse not to check it out.

Booth, Wayne C. "Is There Any Knowledge That A Man Must Have." In The Norton Reader: An Anthology of Expository Prose, edited by Arthur M. Eastman. 7th ed. New York: W.W. Norton & Co, 1988.

Evans, Arthur. Witchcraft and the Gay Counterculture. Boston: Fag Rag Books, 1978. I found out about this book through an excerpt in the magazine Green Anarchy, and I'm so very glad I did. It's a gift, especially his chapter called "Sex among the Zombies." It's an amazing articulation of sexual repression and violence caused by civilization. The address for Fag Rag Books is Box 331, Kenmore Station, Boston, MA 02215.

Farber, Jerry. The Student As Nigger. This one is all over the Internet. Here is one url: http://www.soilandhealth.org/03sov/0303critic/030301studentasnigger.html. It's an amazing essay, as good, I think, as John Taylor Gatto's work. Very powerful. It was written in 1969, but retains all its relevance.

The first lines that I cite as examples of great beginnings I use to inspire myself before I write are from, respectively, R. D. Laing's The Politics of Experience, Harper Lee's To Kill a Mockingbird, Judith Herman's Trauma and Recovery, John Steinbeck's East of Eden (that one's not actually the opener, but the second paragraph), Stephen King's The Body, Arno Gruen's The Betrayal of the Self, and Stanley Diamond's In Search of the Primitive.

Ford, Madox Ford. As with the quotes by Paul O'Neil and Gene Fowler, I got this quote from a nice little handbook entitled A Writer's Notebook: Insights from Writers with Space for Personal Notes. Philadephia: Running Press Book Publishers, 1984.

Fralin, Francis. *The Indelible Image: Photographs of War—1846 to the Present.* New York: Harry N. Abrams, 1985. The Fortino Samano photograph and the photograph of the massacre outside of Kerch are from this book, one of the best collections of war photographs (turned into a very powerful antiwar message) I've ever seen.

Foucault, Michel. *Discipline & Punish: The Birth of the Prison.* Translated by Alan Sheridan. New York: Vintage Books, 1979. Great book about how we live in a society structured such that we constantly police ourselves. This book should be on the top of the reading list for anyone forced to go to school. And so far as his opening to the book, oh my. It's intense. Check it out.

Fowler, Gene. As with the quotes by Ford Madox Ford and Paul O'Neil, I got this quote from a nice little handbook entitled *A Writer's Notebook: Insights From Writers With Space For Personal Notes.* Philadelphia: Running Press Book Publishers, 1984. As is also true for O'Neil, I have no idea who Gene Fowler is.

Galeano, Eduardo. *Memory of Fire. Vol. 3 of Century of the Wind.* Translated by Cedric Belfrage. New York: Pantheon, 1988. Words cannot do this book justice. Galeano is a wonderful writer, maybe my favorite.

Gatto, John Taylor. *The Underground History of American Education: An Intimate Investigation into the Problem of Modern Schooling.* New York: Oxford Village Press, 2001. All of the quotes, from that by the Senate Committee on Education to William Torrey Harris' second quote, are from Gatto. If I were only going to read one book on the problems of education (besides the one you hold in your hands, of course), I think it would be this one. Gatto is unparalleled in his ability to articulate what is wrong with modern schooling, and what can be done about it. If you're into that sort of thing, much of this book can be read online at http://www.johntaylorgatto.com/.

Gruen, Arno. *The Betrayal of the Self: The Fear of Autonomy in Men and Women.* Translated by Hildegaarde and Hunter Hannum. New York: Grove Press, 1988.

———. *The Insanity of Normality: Realism As Sickness: Toward Understanding Human Destructiveness.* Translated by Hildegaarde and Hunter Hannum. New York: Grove Weidenfeld, 1992. Arno Gruen is, I think, the most underrated writer about the destructiveness of the dominant culture.

Henry, Jules. *Culture against Man*. New York: Random House, 1963. This is an important exploration of American culture. My copy has so many scraps of paper marking favorite passages as to render these marks relatively ineffective.

Hesse, Hermann. *Demian*. Translated by Michael Roloff and Michael Lebeck. New York: Bantam Books, 1975. This was the first Hesse I read, and probably my favorite.

"If they give you lined paper, write the other way." I don't know who first said this. I've seen it attributed to Ray Bradbury, William Carlos Williams, e.e. cummings, and Juan Ramón Jiménez. That's one thing that bugs me about the Internet: nobody seems to put full citations (except the wonderful Goethe Society of America!). A pox upon all their houses, and may rats chew their phone lines.

Johnson, Charles. Interview in *At the Field's End: Interviews with 20 Pacific Northwest Writers*, edited by Nicholas O'Connell. Seattle: Madrona Publishers, 1987. My mom got this book for my birthday when I was still counting my words, and when my *being* a writer was still a dream.

Kazantzakis, Nikos. *Zorba the Greek*. Translated by Carl Wildman. New York: Simon and Schuster, 1952.

Keller, Helen. As with the lined paper quote, this one is everywhere on the Internet. But none of the places I've looked give me an original print citation. Sheesh, didn't anybody teach these kids how to do citations??? Where are their teachers? We need to bring back the basics! Oh, sorry, got carried away there.

King, Stephen. *Salem's Lot*. New York: Signet, 1975. I don't think I'm alone in thinking this is one of King's two or three best novels. If you're one of the few people who haven't read one of his books who has any desire to, this might be the place to start, unless vampires scare you too much, in which case you might try *The Dead Zone*, which was, I think, more of a love story than horror.

The Memory Hole. One of many thousands of websites that provide the sort of analysis never found in the mainstream corporate-controlled press or in mainstream corporate-controlled schools. The url is: http://www.thememoryhole.org/. I am often of course classified as a Luddite. Moreso even than that I am often labeled an anarcho-primitivist. Both of these labels fit well enough, I suppose. Be that as it may, there is almost no way I could do the amount of research I need to do and still live in a small town (nearest large library, seventy miles) without the Internet. It's pretty damn handy. Of course without the culture that leads to this technology I wouldn't have to be trying to stop the planet from being killed, and wouldn't have to do this work anyway. The Internet being groovy doesn't alter the fact that we need to bring down civilization.

Murray, W. H. *The Scottish Himalayan Expedition.* London: Dent, 1951. I include this book in reference to the epigraph that opens the chapter "Falling in Love." This quote, usually attributed to Johann Wolfgang von Goethe, is another one that's all over the Internet, and it's all over posters, etc. But it ends up that ol' Johann never actually said it. Here's what I learned at the website of the Goethe Society of America. Someone found "a variant of the final two sentences in Stevenson's *Home Book of Quotations:* 'Boldness has genius, power, and magic in it. Only engage, and then the mind grows heated. Begin it, and the work will be completed.' The lines are attributed to John Anster in a 'very free translation' of *Faust* from 1835." The website provides the original German text to prove how free it is. Unfortunately my five years of German in junior high and high school doesn't get me much past asking "Is Erika at home?" and answering "Yes, she is upstairs," so I can't verify the freeness of the translation. (This seems as good a place as any to mention a trick played on us students by our German reading teacher in eleventh grade. Our first German book was *Winnie the Pooh,* followed by *Emil and the Detectives.* After that she jumped us right to Franz Kafka's *The Metamorphosis.* I read the entire story convinced that the first sentence, in which Gregor Samsa awakens as a cockroach, was an obscure German idiomatic expression meaning he's in a really bad mood.) The website then goes on to say that the quote is actually from Murray: "But when I said that nothing had been done I erred in one important matter. We had definitely committed ourselves and were halfway out of our ruts. We had put down our passage money—booked a sailing to Bombay. This may sound too simple, but is great in consequence. Until one is committed, there is hesitancy, the chance to draw back, always ineffectiveness. Concerning all acts of initiative (and creation), there is one elementary truth the ignorance of which kills countless ideas and splendid plans: that the moment one definitely commits oneself, the providence moves too. A whole stream of events issues from the decision, raising in one's favor all manner of unforeseen incidents, meetings and material assistance, which no man could have dreamt would have come his way. I learned a deep respect for one of Goethe's couplets: Whatever you can do or dream you can, begin it. Boldness has genius, power and magic in it!" Cool, eh? The website is http://www. goethesociety.org/pages/quotescom.html. Another thing I need to mention is that when I do a Google search for the phrase, "Boldness has genius, power and magic in it," one of the hits that comes up is an advertisement that says, "Male Boldness a concern? New clinically proven hair grown system to help with male boldness."

O'Neil, Paul. As with the quotes by Ford Madox Ford and Gene Fowler, I got this quote from a nice little handbook entitled *A Writer's Notebook: Insights From Writers With Space For Personal Notes*. Philadelphia: Running Press Book Publishers, 1984. I must admit I have no idea who Paul O'Neil is. I'm presuming it is neither Paul O'Neill the U. S. Secretary of the Treasury nor Paul O'Neill the former right fielder for the New York Yankees.

Pink Floyd. The song "Time" is by Roger Waters, from the album/CD *The Dark Side of the Moon*, Capitol Records, 1973.

Rogers, Carl. *On Becoming a Person*. Boston: Houghton Mifflin, 1961. My mom got this book for a psychology class she took in the 1970s. Somehow the book migrated to my bookshelves, and remained there unread for years. For some unknown reason I picked it up the very evening before I was to first enter the classroom at Eastern Washington University, and read through most of it that night. Although it's a long book and I was getting tired by the time I got to his very short chapter on education, his words woke me right back up. I've never before or since read any better description of what it means to be a "teacher." This is why the working title of my book was *How To Not Teach*.

Trumbo, Dalton. *johnny got his gun*. New York: Bantam, 1970. Easily the best antiwar novel I've ever read, and one of the best novels. Trumbo's style influenced me deeply.

Williams, Terry Tempest. *Desert Quartet: An Erotic Landscape.* New York: Pantheon Books, 1995. Terry Tempest Williams is a stunning writer and an even more stunning speaker. If you ever have a chance to hear her talk, do so.